# THE GIST OF IT

## RODNEY LEE

Fishamble Theatre Company is funded by
The Arts Council/An Chomhairle Ealaíon and Dublin City Council.

## FISHAMBLE

## FISHAMBLE WISHES TO THANK THE FOLLOWING FRIENDS OF FISHAMBLE FOR THEIR INVALUABLE SUPPORT

Robert & Lilian Chambers
Helen Cunningham
Brian Friel
Hugh Gaffney
Marian Keyes
Maureen McGlynn & Eleanor Minihan
Vincent O'Doherty
Andrew & Delyth Parkes
Lisa Richards

Thank you also to those who do not wish to be credited.

For details on how to become a Friend of Fishamble please see www.fishamble.com or send an email to info@fishamble.com

## FISHAMBLE ALSO WISHES TO THANK THE FOLLOWING FOR THEIR SUPPORT WITH *THE GIST OF IT*

Willie White, Niamh O'Donnell, Dairne O'Sullivan and all at Project, Brid Dukes and all at the Civic Theatre, Enid Reid Whyte, John O'Kane and all at The Arts Council, Jack Gilligan and all at Dublin City Council Arts Office, Bert and all at the IFI, Hilda Doyle, Marie Kelly, Aaron Monaghan, Karl Shiels, David Parnell, Siobhán Ní Chonchúir at IES, Nick Hern and all at Nick Hern Books, Avril Carr at The Ark, Theresa & Stephen Lee, Brendan O'Connell, Patrick Sutton and the students of The Gaiety School of Acting, Theresa Ebenhoeh, Eoghan Doyle, Stuart McLaughlin, Jenny Sherwin at Wicklow County Council, and all those who have helped Fishamble with the production since this publication went to print.

# THE GIST OF IT

by Rodney Lee

*The Gist of It* premiered at Project Arts Centre,
Dublin, on 23rd February 2006.

*The play is set in a house in present day Dublin.*
*Act 1 takes place on Saturday afternoon,*
*Act 2 on Saturday evening and Act 3 on Sunday morning.*

*The performance runs for approximately 90 minutes with no interval.*

## CAST IN ORDER OF APPEARANCE

| | |
|---|---|
| LIAM | **PAUL REID** |
| ORLA | **AMY CONROY** |
| GERARD | **PHILIP O'SULLIVAN** |
| | |
| DIRECTOR | **JIM CULLETON** |
| DESIGNER | **SONIA HACCIUS** |
| LIGHTING DESIGNER | **SINEAD MCKENNA** |
| SOUND DESIGNERS/COMPOSERS | **IVAN BIRTHISTLE** |
| | **VINCENT DOHERTY** |
| PROJECTION DESIGNER | **ONE PRODUCTIONS** |
| PRODUCER | **ORLA FLANAGAN** |
| PRODUCTION MANAGER | **DES KENNY** |
| STAGE DIRECTOR | **ANNE LAYDE** |
| STAGE MANAGER | **AINE BEAMISH** |
| STAGE MANAGEMENT INTERN | **THERESA EBENHOEH** |
| ASSISTANT DIRECTOR INTERN | **EOGHAN DOYLE** |
| SCRIPT DEVELOPMENT | **GAVIN KOSTICK** |
| PR/MARKETING | **CERSTIN MUDIWA** |
| PHOTOGRAPHY | **COLM HOGAN** |
| GRAPHIC DESIGNER | **GARETH JONES** |
| PRINTERS | **CUNNINGHAM PRINTERS** |
| VOICEOVERS | **STUDENTS OF THE GAIETY SCHOOL OF ACTING** |

*Please note that the text of the play which appears in this volume may be changed during the rehearsal process and appear in a slightly altered form in performance.*

## ABOUT FISHAMBLE

The Company was founded in 1988 and, since 1990, has been dedicated to the discovery, development and production of new work for the Irish stage. Formerly known as Pigsback, the Company was renamed Fishamble in 1997. The name is inspired by Dublin's Fishamble Street and in particular, its playhouse which, in 1784, became the first Irish theatre to pursue a policy of producing solely new Irish work.

Fishamble has produced a number of plays by first-time and established playwrights in Dublin, throughout Ireland, in transfers to Britain (including London's Tricycle, Edinburgh's Traverse and Glasgow's Tron) and on tour internationally. The Company has won and been nominated for numerous prestigious awards including *The Irish Times*/ESB Theatre Awards, BBC/Stewart Parker Trust Awards, Croatia International Radio Festival Awards, *In Dublin* Awards and Entertainment & Media Awards.

As part of its commitment to developing new work for the theatre, Fishamble regularly presents workshops, discussions and seminars, as well as in-house and public readings of new work. New work currently in development includes plays by Pat Kinevane, Gary Duggan, Sean McLoughlin and Gavin Kostick. Fishamble runs a number of playwriting courses and workshops which are open to the public; *The Gist of It* emerged following Rodney Lee's participation in a Fishamble writers' course. These courses take place regularly – for more information email the Literary Officer, Gavin Kostick, at gavin@fishamble.com.

*The Gist of It* is part of the Company's *Fishamble Firsts* series, which most recently included Gary Duggan's first play, *Monged*, and also includes Sean McLoughlin's first play, *Noah and the Tower Flower*, which is currently under development. Fishamble recently received hundreds of short plays in response to its *Do You Have Something to Tell Me?* call for submissions. The selected plays will be presented as site-specific productions during summer 2006, as part of Temple Bar's *Diversions*. Fishamble is also working with Tinderbox Theatre Company and director Annabelle Comyn on *Express* - a major event involving playwriting workshops for young people on both sides of the border.

Fishamble often works in partnership with other arts and non-arts organisations. Recent and current partners include venues and festivals throughout Ireland, as well as Amnesty International, RTE lyric fm, British Council Ireland, International Theatre Festival of Sibiu, Prague Fringe Festival, TNL Canada, Ireland Newfoundland Partnership, New Island Books, TCD School of Drama, The Gaiety School of Acting, NAYD, Tinderbox Theatre Company, Business-2-Arts, 7:84 Scotland, Stellar Quines, Dundee Rep, Traverse Theatre, Playwrights' Studio Scotland, National Theatre of Scotland, Accenture and Temple Bar Properties.

'Fishamble puts electricity into the National grid of dreams.' Sebastian Barry

'Jim Culleton's work with new playwrights at Fishamble has detonated a controlled explosion of fresh talent.' Fintan O'Toole

# PRODUCTIONS TO DATE

## 2005
**55° and rising:** a reading series of Scottish plays by Stephen Greenhorn, David Harrower, David Greig and Zinnie Harris
**Monged** by Gary Duggan
**She Was Wearing...** by Sebastian Barry, Maeve Binchy, Dermot Bolger, Michael Collins, Stella Feehily, Rosalind Haslett, Roisin Ingle, Marian Keyes and Gavin Kostick

## 2004
**Pilgrims in the Park** by Jim O'Hanlon
**Tadhg Stray Wandered In** by Michael Collins
**Dislocated:** a reading series of plays by Marius von Mayenburg, Benny McDonnell and Leo Butler

## 2003
A season of radio plays: **Handel's Crossing** by Joe O'Connor, **The Medusa** by Gavin Kostick, **Chaste Diana** by Michael West, **Sweet Bitter** by Stella Feehily
**Shorts: All the Glove in the World** by Dawn Bradfield, **Mary Quirke** by Aino Dubrawsky, **Meeting Venus** by Simon O'Gorman, **The Wedding Dance** by Ciara Considine, **The Journey** by Tina Reilly, **Moira** by Mary Portser, **The Killers** by Colm Maher, **Awimbawey** by James Heaney, **Tara Has Written a Play** by Tara Dairman, **The Naked Truth** by Lorraine McArdle, **The Burial** by Talaya Delaney, **Voice** by Ger Gleeson, **Game** by Stella Feehily, **A New Suit** by Bryan Delaney
**The Buddhist of Castleknock** by Jim O'Hanlon (revival)

## 2002
**Contact** by Jeff Pitcher and Gavin Kostick
**The Buddhist of Castleknock** by Jim O'Hanlon
**Still** by Rosalind Haslett

## 2001
**The Carnival King** by Ian Kilroy
**Wired to the Moon** by Maeve Binchy, adapted by Jim Culleton

## 2000
**Y2K Festival: Consenting Adults** by Dermot Bolger, **Dreamframe** by Deirdre Hines, **Moonlight and Music** by Jennifer Johnston, **The Great Jubilee** by Nicholas Kelly, **Doom Raider** by Gavin Kostick, **Tea Set** by Gina Moxley

## 1999
**The Plains of Enna** by Pat Kinevane
**True Believers** by Joe O'Connor

## 1998
**The Nun's Wood** by Pat Kinevane

## 1997
**From Both Hips** by Mark O'Rowe

## 1996
**The Flesh Addict** by Gavin Kostick

## 1995
**Sardines** by Michael West
**Red Roses and Petrol** by Joe O'Connor

## 1994
**Jack Ketch's Gallows Jig** by Gavin Kostick

## 1993
**Buffalo Bill Has Gone To Alaska** by Colin Teevan
**The Ash Fire** by Gavin Kostick (revival)

## 1992
**The Ash Fire** by Gavin Kostick
**The Tender Trap** by Michael West

## 1991
**Howling Moons/Silent Sons** by Deirdre Hines
**This Love Thing** by Marina Carr

## 1990
**Don Juan** by Michael West

# FISHAMBLE PUBLICATIONS

**Fishamble/Pigsback: First Plays** - published by New Island Books and edited by Jim Culleton, with a preface by Dermot Bolger, this anthology includes *Howling Moons, Silent Sons* by Deirdre Hines, *The Ash Fire* by Gavin Kostick, *Red Roses and Petrol* by Joseph O'Connor, *From Both Hips* by Mark O'Rowe, *The Nun's Wood* by Pat Kinevane and *The Carnival King* by Ian Kilroy.
**Shorts,** a collection of short plays and **Tadhg Stray Wandered In** by Michael Collins - published by Fishamble and available from the Company.
**Red Roses and Petrol** by Joseph O'Connor - published by Methuen.
**From Both Hips** by Mark O'Rowe - published by Nick Hern Books.
**The Nun's Wood** by Pat Kinevane, **Still** by Rosalind Haslett and **The Medusa** by Gavin Kostick - published by the International Festival of Sibiu in English and Romanian.
**The Buddhist of Castleknock** by Jim O'Hanlon - due to be published in spring 2006 by New Island Books.

*(left to right) PHILIP O'SULLIVAN, AMY CONROY, PAUL REID* (photographs by Colm Hogan)

## AMY CONROY ORLA

Amy trained at the Core School of Theatre Studies for three years. Since graduating in 1999 her roles have included Clytemnestra in *The Agamemnon*, Martha/Philip in *The Mysteries 2000*, Monk in *Dreaming of the Bones* and understudy to Anna Manahan in the Irish tour of *The Matchmaker*, all with The Machine Theatre Company. Other works include *The Country Woman* (Upstate Theatre Project), *Angelene* (Aistir Theatre Company), *Reverse Psychology* (Daghdha Dance Company) as part of the International Dance Festival Ireland, *The BFG* (Civic Theatre), *Don't Take Your Coat Off* (Darkhorse Theatre Company) and an Irish tour of *Bumbogs and Bees* (TEAM Educational Theatre Company). Amy has also worked with Barabbas...The Company in *Blowfish*, including an Irish and Northern Irish tour, *Parable of the Plums* for ReJoyce Dublin 2004, and most recently *Luca* in Project Arts Centre. She has just finished *Displaced* with Anonymous Theatre Company and is delighted to be working with Fishamble.

## PHILIP O'SULLIVAN GERARD

Philip O'Sullivan was a member of the Abbey Theatre Company from 1973-77 and from 1979-84. Productions in that time included *Oedipus, Mrs. Warren's Profession, Hamlet, Measure for Measure, The Vicar of Wakefield, Mary Makebelieve, The Glass Menagerie, Hidden Curriculum, The Plough and the Stars, The Hard Life* and *Sanctified Distances*. Appearances at other theatres include *One Flew over the Cuckoo's Nest* (Pearson Productions), *Love for Love* (Smock Alley), *You Never Can Tell, Hay Fever, Jennifer's Vacation, Tartuffe, A Tale of Two Cities, Lady Windemere's Fan* (Gate). More recent theatre appearances include *The Misanthrope*

by Moliere (Gate), *A Delicate Balance* by Edward Albee (Focus), *Come Up and See Me Sometime* (Pavilion), *The Dock Brief* by John Mortimer (Bewleys Café Theatre), *Olga* by Laura Ruohonen (Rough Magic), Peter Schaffer's *Amadeus* (Theatreworks – Ouroboros), *The Goat* by Edward Albee (Landmark), Brian Friel's *Making History* (Ouroboros), *How Many Miles to Babylon* by Jennifer Johnston (Second Age). Philip also directed Carl Djerassi's *Calculus* for the Einstein Year at the Schrödinger Theatre (TCD). TV and film roles include *Sean, Teresa's Wedding, The Burke Enigma, Leave it to Mrs. O'Brien, Eagles & Trumpets, SOS Titanic, The Ambassador, The American, Anytime Now, Veronica Guerin, The Return, Tristan & Isolde* and five years as Fr. Tracey in *Glenroe*. Also *Showbands* (RTE/Parallel), *The League of Gentlemen's Apocalypse* (Ch. 4 UK), *The Baby War* (Granada UK), *Pure Mule* (RTE), *Studs* by Paul Mercier (Brother Films) and *Showbands 2* (RTE/ Parallel). This is Philip's first engagement with Fishamble.

## PAUL REID LIAM

Born in Dublin, Paul graduated from the Gaiety School of Acting full time diploma course in June 2004. Since then he has appeared in *Love Is The Drug* as Toby, directed by Darren Thornton (Rough Magic Films/RTE 2), and as Shane in Stephen Bradley's feature film *Boy Eats Girl* (Element Films). Paul made his theatre debut shortly after leaving college in *Pilgrims in the Park*, directed by Jim Culleton for Fishamble Theatre Company and shortly afterwards appeared in their hugely popular production of *Monged* by Gary Duggan, also directed by Jim Culleton, at Project Arts Centre. Most recently Paul appeared as Rodolpho in Mark Brokaw's highly acclaimed production of *A View From the Bridge* by Arthur Miller at the Gate Theatre.

**RODNEY LEE** AUTHOR

After completing a BA in philosophy and linguistics at University College Dublin, Rodney studied film and television in Dun Laoghaire Institute of Art, Design and Technology. He produced, lit, wrote and directed his own graduate film *Edge of Destruction*. This black comedy was screened at the Cork, Galway and Brest Film Festivals. After leaving college Rodney worked for many years as an editor but after winning the Tiernan McBride Screenwriting Award in 2004, he is now writing for the stage and screen full-time. His credits include *Autograph* (Lyric FM radio-play, 2004) and the short film *Nun More Deadly* (Winner of Sligo Film Festival Best Short 2005). In 2005, he also won the WYD-Eye international script competition. *The Gist of It* is Rodney's first stage play.

**JIM CULLETON** DIRECTOR

Jim Culleton is the Artistic Director of Fishamble for which he most recently directed *Monged* by Gary Duggan, *She Was Wearing...* by Sebastian Barry, Maeve Binchy, Dermot Bolger, Michael Collins, Stella Feehily, Rosalind Haslett, Roisin Ingle, Marian Keyes and Gavin Kostick for Amnesty International, *Pilgrims in the Park* by Jim O'Hanlon, *Tadhg Stray Wandered In* by Michael Collins and four radio plays by Joe O'Connor, Gavin Kostick, Michael West and Stella Feehily in association with RTE lyric fm. He has also directed for Pigsback, 7:84 (Scotland), Project Arts Centre, Amharclann de hIde, Tinderbox, The Passion Machine, The Ark, Second Age, The Abbey & Peacock, Semper Fi, TNL Canada, Scotland's Ensemble @ Dundee Rep, Draiocht, Barnstorm and the TCD School of Drama. He co-edited *Contemporary Irish Monologues* and edited *Fishamble/Pigsback: First Plays* both for New Island Books and has edited/contributed to books for Carysfort Press, Ubu and Amnesty International.

**SONIA HACCIUS** DESIGNER

Sonia Haccius took an M.A. in set design at the Slade School of Fine Art in London. She has subsequently designed sets for Focus Theatre, Rattlebag, Barnstorm, Peri-Talking, Island Theatre Company and the Abbey Theatre as well as *Rigoletto* for Co-Opera Company. Productions abroad include *The Importance of Being Earnest* and *The Ghosts of Poe*, and *Romeo and Juliet* in Germany. Film and television work includes *Olive, Right Now Ladies and Gents, You're A Star* and the O2 Ability Awards. Sonia has also designed and produced several exhibitions for heritage centres, including the Dunbrody Famine Ship and Belvedere House.

**SINEAD MCKENNA** LIGHTING DESIGNER

Sinead Mckenna graduated from Trinity College in 2000 where she studied Drama and Theatre. Most recent theatre designs include *The Snow Queen* and *Merry Christmas Betty Ford* (Lyric Theatre), *How Many Miles to Babylon* (Second Age), *Wunderkind* (Calypo), *Shooting Gallery* (Bedrock), the musical *Improbable Frequency* (Rough Magic/ The Abbey Theatre), *Oliver* (The Helix/ Cork Opera House), *No Messin With The Monkeys* and *Rudolf The Red'* (The Ark), *Boston Marriage* (B'Spoke), *Hard to Believe* and *Hansel and Gretel* (Storytellers), *The Woman who Walked into Doors* (Joe O'Byrne/ Roddy Doyle) and *Finders Keepers* (Peacock Theatre). For Semper Fi she designed *Adrenalin* and *Ladies and Gents* for which she won the the *The Irish Times* ESB Theatre Award for 'Best Lighting Design'. For Guna Nua she designed *Skin Deep* (nominated 'Best Lighting Design' The *Irish Times* ESB Theatre Awards 2003), *Scenes from a Watercooler, The Real Thing* and *'Dinner with Friends'*. For The Performance Corporation she designed *Candide* and *The Butterfly Ranch*. Dance designs include *Swept* ( CoisCeim/ Abbey Theatre), and *As a Matter of Fact* (Dance Theatre of Ireland). Other dance designs include *Buttons* and *Suil Eile* for Fluxus Dance. She designed the opera *La Boheme* for Co-Opera.

**VINCENT DOHERTY AND IVAN BIRTHISTLE**
SOUND DESIGNERS/COMPOSERS

Vincent has been working as a freelance sound designer and composer for the last few years. He has also been involved in a series of collaborations with, among others, Ivan Birthistle and Daniel Figgis. Recent theatre sound designs include *Mud, Foley*, and *Lolita* for The Corn Exchange Theatre, *Blasted* and *Night Just Before the Forest* for Bedrock Productions, *Three Days of Rain* for Rough Magic Theatre Company, *Still* for Fishamble Theatre Company, *What the Dead Want* by Alex Johnston, *Elysian Juniors* by Ken Harmon, *Aoife & Isobel* by Gavin Kostick and *The Mai* by Marina Carr. Also for Semper Fi he composed for *24 Hours of Dance.* Ivan Birthistle has been working in the music industry for the last thirteen years and in theatre for the last five. He currently plays keyboards and guitar with Nina Hynes. He is also Music Director with Semper Fi (Ireland). Designs for Semper Fi include *Ladies and Gents* by Paul Walker, *Ten* by Eugene O'Brien, *Butterflies* by Ian McEwan, *Breakfast With Versace* and *Within 24 Hours of Dance.* Other sound designs include *African Voices, The Gods Are Not To Blame* and *Once Upon a Time* for (Arambe), *Doldrum Bay* (Peacock), *Bloodknot* (South Africa Week at the Helix), *The White Piece* (I.M.D.T.).

Vincent and Ivan decided to pool their talents and now work on an ongoing collaborative basis, past work includes *Shooting Gallery, Far Away, The Massacre @ Paris*, and *Feint*, all for Bedrock, and *Adrenalin* and *Slaughter* (Pan Pan Theatre Symposium) for Semper Fi. Also *Not So Long Ago* (Arambe), *My Children! My Africa* (Gallowglass), *True West, Shadow of a Gunman* (Lyric Theatre), *Tadhg Stray Wandered In, Monged* (Fishamble), *Universal Export, Whose House?, A/S/L* (Gaiety School) and *Luca* (Barabbas).

## ONE PRODUCTIONS  PROJECTION DESIGNER
One Productions is a production company founded in 2000 to produce quality film and television content and to provide services in the media sector. In addition, One Productions also produces content for music, fashion, publishing, mobile and the web. One Production's short films, *Close, O* and *Money, Fear and Justice* have appeared at many prestigious international festivals including Venice, Montreal, Palm Springs, New York, Sao Paolo and Clermont-Ferrand. These films have also been nominated for digital media awards in 2006. One Productions also developed and co-produced *Skin Deep* with Guna Nua, an award-winning play, which was nominated for two *The Irish Times* ESB Theatre Awards in 2004.

## ORLA FLANAGAN  PRODUCER
Orla has recently joined Fishamble as General Manager. Prior to this she was the Literary Officer at the Abbey Theatre since 2001. She has also worked as Marketing Administrator at the National Concert Hall and has produced a number of shows for the Dublin Fringe Festival. In 2005 she worked as a trainee dramaturg at the Sundance Theatre Lab, Utah, and the Schaubuhne's Festival of International New Drama 05, Berlin.

## DES KENNY  PRODUCTION MANAGER
Recent credits include *Pilgrims in the Park, Tadhg Stray Wandered In* and *Monged* for Fishamble, *Far Away, Urban Ghosts* and *Shooting Gallery* for Bedrock, *Alone It Stands* for Lane Productions and Yew Tree Theatre Company, *Triple Espresso* for Lane Productions, *Dublin by Lamplight* and *Mud* for The Corn Exchange and *How Many Miles to Babylon* and *Macbeth* for Second Age.

## ANNE LAYDE  STAGE DIRECTOR
Anne Layde has worked extensively in Dublin as a stage manager. Anne had the opportunity to work abroad on shows produced by the Abbey and Gate Theatres, which toured to London and New York. She worked as Production Stage Manager on part of the European and New York run of *Riverdance*. This is Anne's first time to work with Fishamble Theatre Company, and she is delighted to be part of the production of *The Gist of It*.

## AINE BEAMISH  STAGE MANAGER
Previous theatre works includes the recent Pinter Festival, *A View from the Bridge, Poor Beast in the Rain* and *Shining City* at the Gate Theatre. Aine has a BA(hons) in Digital Media from the University of Wolverhampton. Other production work includes Dublin Theatre Festival, St. Patrick's Festival, Festival of World Culture and Dublin Fringe Festival. This is Aine's first production with Fishamble.

## GAVIN KOSTICK  SCRIPT DEVELOPMENT
Gavin Kostick is Literary Officer with Fishamble. In this role, he works with new writers for theatre through development meetings, readings and a variety of courses. He is also involved in encouraging new ways of thinking about theatre production. Gavin is also an award-winning playwright. He has written around a dozen plays which have been produced in Dublin, on tour around Ireland, the UK, New York and Philadelphia. He is currently working with the Gaiety School of Acting on a version of *Tales of Ovid* and a new play, *A Play About Us,* for Fishamble.

## CERSTIN MUDIWA  PR/MARKETING
As Fishamble's PR & Marketing Officer, Cerstin publicised *The Carnival King* by Ian Kilroy, *Still* by Rosalind Haslett, *The Buddhist of Castleknock* and *Pilgrims in the Park* by Jim O'Hanlon, *Shorts,* The RTE lyric fm/Fishamble season of four new radio plays, *Tadhg Stray Wandered In* by Michael Collins, *She Was Wearing...* for Amnesty's International Women's Day Festival and *Monged* by Gary Duggan. Her work as a freelance publicist includes *Two Magpies* by Abbie Spallen, *The Country* for Hatch Productions and for The Performance Corporation *The Seven Deadly Sins, The Butterfly Ranch, The Irish Times* Theatre Award winning *Candide* and *Dr. Ledbetter's Experiment* and most recently *The Yokohama Delegation.* She also worked with a number of bands as a tour manager and booking agent in Ireland and continental Europe.

# THE GIST OF IT

Rodney Lee

*To Theresa and Stephen Lee*

**Characters**

ORLA CULLEN, *a film student in her early twenties*

LIAM DUFFY, *a film student in his early twenties*

GERARD CULLEN, *Orla's father, an English teacher in his forties*

## ACT ONE

*Saturday afternoon. Coloured lights flash on the stage in time
to atonal music. The sound of a baby crying plays over the
music. Images are projected onto the walls; a close-up of
butterfly wings, a worm crawling on an apple, a cow's heart in
liquid. A spotlight illuminates an old Victorian dollhouse in the
centre of the stage. LIAM, in a white shirt, appears behind it.
He holds up a large plastic butterfly and walks around the
dollhouse.*

LIAM.
> She has no future, no chance . . .
> To soar her wings will become . . . dust.
> Behind a locked door, her heart is no more worn out by strife.
> Her taciturn scream lost . . .
> In the night, no more . . .
> Dreams know nothing . . .
> Know life . . .

> LIAM *pulls the plastic butterfly apart. A voice is heard from
> the darkness.*

ORLA. No, no, no.

LIAM (*weary*). Jesus.

ORLA. That . . .

LIAM. What?

ORLA. Hmm . . .

LIAM (*shrugs*). What?

ORLA. I don't . . . (*Tries to find the words.*)

LIAM. Don't what?

ORLA. It was . . . (*Tries to find the words.*)

LIAM. Christ, Orla, come on.

LIAM *holds up a clapperboard before the camera.*

Do you want an end-board?

ORLA. Don't bother.

ORLA *turns on the lights to reveal the ground floor of a small house. On the left, a living room. On the right, a kitchen.*

*In the living room, on the right, there's a sofa at an angle, a small TV and video facing it and a coffee table beside it. A coat rack and waste-paper bin stand beside the door. A video camera on a tripod is pointed at an angle in front of* LIAM. *The room is cluttered with film-making equipment, props, etc. In the corner, against the wall is a shelf of videotapes, most with handwritten labels, others are unlabelled. In another corner is a fish tank filled with liquid. A cow's heart is suspended in it.*

*In the kitchen, there's a table and chair. On the table is a telephone. At the back is a sink and washboard.*

*The door, left, leads to the hallway.*

ORLA (*sighs*). What am I going to do?

LIAM. What are *you* going to do? Just tell me . . .

ORLA. It's not that easy, Liam.

LIAM. Tell me how you want me to say it. What's the big deal?

ORLA. That had no . . . (*Struggles to find the words.*)

LIAM. No what?

ORLA. No biological necessity.

LIAM. What?

ORLA. Make it more coruscating. Think about feelings of intense pain, sorrow, etcetera.

LIAM. What are you saying?

ORLA. Undulating anguish.

LIAM. Huh?

ORLA. You're too emotionally prosaic. You're not thinking about the meaning behind the words.

LIAM. What meaning!?

LIAM *plonks down on the sofa, exhausted.*

ORLA. If you'd only do what I wrote in the script.

LIAM. I'm not doing that.

ORLA. The way I originally envisioned it.

LIAM. No.

ORLA. It's only a little one.

LIAM (*firm*). I said no.

ORLA. It's Nicole, isn't it?

LIAM. What's Nicole?

ORLA. Why you can't concentrate. It must have been upsetting.

LIAM. Drop it, Orla.

ORLA. I've touched a nerve, I'm backing off.

LIAM. Orla, I couldn't give a toss!

ORLA *lifts up a jar containing a live butterfly.*

ORLA. It probably won't even live that much longer. Butterflies have a very short life-span.

LIAM. Orla, I'm not killing it! How can you be so blasé about killing a butterfly for a student movie?

ORLA. Liam, while, from your point of view, this is only a student film, it's also a work of art and there's no point doing it if you're not going to commit 100 per cent.

LIAM. I don't just mean student movies. I mean killing something for *any movie* is wrong.

ORLA. I'm not making *any movie*.

LIAM (*tired*). I don't see how it helps my performance if I kill an innocent little butterfly anyway.

ORLA. It will help, Liam, because every time you say the speech you have all the gravitas of a sock-puppet. Killing the butterfly will add the extra . . . frisson of existentialism you lack.

LIAM. But it's not just a prop, Orla, it's alive.

ORLA. Look at it this way. If you don't kill it now, it'll only get eaten by a hungry rottweiler or stamped on by some delinquent child.

LIAM. How can someone who cried at *E.T.* be so cynical?

ORLA (*shocked*). I didn't cry at *E.T.*

LIAM. Yes you did. In Larry's class last Tuesday.

ORLA. Right, Liam, a bug-eyed plastic turd on a magic bike truly makes my eyes water.

LIAM. I saw you.

ORLA. No, you didn't.

    LIAM *picks up a biscuit off the table and takes a bite.*

LIAM. Orla, you were weeping like a baby.

ORLA (*annoyed*). Can you not eat when you're wearing that shirt, Liam? You'll get it dirty.

    LIAM *slowly puts the rest of the biscuit down with over-exaggerated care.*

    Oh, and before I forget, 'taciturn' sounds wrong coming out of your mouth. Like a retarded infant learning to speak. Can you practice saying it, please?

LIAM (*sighs*). Look, okay. Let's try this again. This scene is the climax of the movie, is it?

ORLA. It's not a movie, it's a film.

LIAM. Alright, Orla.

    ORLA *sits beside* LIAM, *who flicks through a script.*

ORLA. This is the emotional apotheosis of the film. Broken
    Doll has spent her entire life trying to please Man in White,
    trying to placate him and cater to his whims but of course,
    he barely registers her existence.

LIAM. Why don't I have a name?

ORLA. What?

LIAM. Why am I Man in White? Why amn't I Tony or Donald
    or . . . Ruddeger?

ORLA. You don't have a name because you're not a real
    person.

LIAM. I'm not?

ORLA. No.

LIAM. What am I then?

ORLA. A Jungian construct.

LIAM (*nods, taking this in his stride*). Go on.

ORLA. So Broken Doll returns home during the lunar eclipse
    only to find Man in White about to kill her butterfly. She
    cries out to stop him but her mouth falls off, which was the
    bit we shot this morning, and Man in White kills the
    butterfly. Broken Doll is shattered. She is desolate . . . She
    reverts to a pre-birth state of innocence and denial.

    *A beat.* LIAM *stares at* ORLA *like she's crazy.*

LIAM (*perplexed*). How do you plan on filming a pre-birth
    state of innocence and denial?

ORLA. By showing her blackened heart enveloped in amniotic
    fluid.

LIAM (*pointing to the tank in the corner*). Oh, I get it! That's
    what the cow's heart in brine is all about.

ORLA (*annoyed*). It's not brine, it's amniotic fluid . . . So what
    else do you not understand?

LIAM (*thinks about it, then*). Well . . . what's the point in the
    butterfly?

ORLA. It supports a multitude of readings.

LIAM. Yeah, but . . . what does it represent?

ORLA. Whatever you want it to.

LIAM. That makes no sense.

ORLA. Life doesn't make sense. My art reflects that.

LIAM *stares at her blankly.* ORLA *stands up and goes to the camera.*

You've no idea, Liam, have you? Can't see beyond Friday night down the multiplex? Art is not the same thing as a Sandra Bullock movie.

LIAM. What's wrong with Sandra Bullock?

ORLA. I don't even know how to begin answering that!

LIAM. But how do you expect the audience to get anything from it if it doesn't even make sense?

ORLA. I'm not trying to sell popcorn, Liam. This is not about entertainment, it's about expressing something of the human soul.

LIAM. But what's the point in making a movie if no one gets it? Aren't you trying to communicate something? I mean, isn't that the point?

ORLA (*confident*). My art will find its audience.

LIAM. Not if no one can understand it.

ORLA. I can't believe you of all people are giving me lessons on film-making. By rights you shouldn't still be in the class.

LIAM, *uneasy, gets up and walks away from* ORLA.

LIAM. I never asked them to take me back . . .

ORLA. The only reason you're still here is because you can tell funny jokes and can drink a flaming sambuca while it's on fire. It is not because you know anything about making films. I, on the other hand, do.

ORLA *tosses the jar to* LIAM.

LIAM. I said no . . . Look, I know I've done some stupid things in my time but I'm not the kind of person who kills things on camera.

ORLA. No one in the class will even know. You don't have to worry about that.

LIAM. That's not the point, Orla. It's wrong.

ORLA. What do you mean?

LIAM. What d'you mean what do I mean? And of course the class'll know. It'll be on camera.

ORLA. They're not going to watch my film.

LIAM. It'll be in the graduate screening with the rest of them. Everyone'll see it.

ORLA. I'm sure they'll all pop out for a cigarette when mine is on.

LIAM. No, they'll watch it just to laugh at me.

ORLA. Well, I won't tell them if you don't.

LIAM *holds up the butterfly and studies it.* ORLA *walks up to him.*

(*Impassioned.*) Don't you think it would prefer to die for something important if it had the chance? Art is categorically the most important tool we have for expressing ourselves. Articulating the hidden depths of the unconscious, and preserving that, beyond time and space itself. Doesn't that sound important to you?

LIAM. It's already dead.

LIAM *shakes the jar. The butterfly doesn't move.*

ORLA. What? Let me see!

ORLA *snatches the jar off him, sits down and examines it.*

LIAM. You really should've put air-holes in it . . .

ORLA *prods the butterfly.*

ORLA. Fuck! Don't do this to me. This scene is crucial!

LIAM *strolls over to the dollhouse and picks up a piece of tiny furniture.* ORLA *glances at him.*

I told you not to touch that, Liam. It's only borrowed and it's very, very expensive!

LIAM. Okay.

LIAM *walks away from it.*

(*Annoyed.*) I can see why your original actor dropped out.

ORLA. His wife went into labour in a Dunnes Stores.

LIAM (*overlapping*). . . . labour in a Dunnes Stores. I know. Very believable.

ORLA (*re: butterfly*). It moved! It's still alive. I'll let it breathe for a while.

ORLA *puts the jar on the coffee table and covers it loosely.*

And for your information, it's true. He spent hours on the phone telling me how guilty he felt. I practically had to convince him not to call around.

LIAM. Okay, fair enough. He was telling the truth.

ORLA. Why would he have lied anyway?

LIAM (*mutters*). Has he read the script?

ORLA *glares at* LIAM, *offended by his comment. She goes back to the camera.*

ORLA (*casually*). I wonder what Nicole's up to tonight? . . . Probably off into town with Bonnie and Miriam. Maybe Copperface Jacks? . . . All dressed up . . . On the pull . . .

LIAM *glares at* ORLA. *A beat.*

LIAM. Y'know, it's funny. All this time I've been wondering why I wasn't able to get your movie. I thought it was becoz I was thick but I just realised. The problem isn't me – (*He picks up the script.*) it's your script. I don't understand it coz there's nothing to understand. It's just meaningless wank about nothing.

LIAM *tosses the script on the sofa.* ORLA *doesn't respond.* LIAM, *tired and frustrated, walks away from her. He takes*

*off the white shirt he's been wearing and hangs it over the
sofa. Topless, he looks around for his T-shirt.* ORLA *silently
watches him. He finds it and puts it on, then goes back to
eating his biscuit.*

ORLA. Liam, why are you here?

LIAM. Huh?

ORLA. Why did you agree to help me?

LIAM (*uncomfortable*). I told you . . .

ORLA. What?

LIAM. You needed an actor so . . . that's why.

ORLA. All of a sudden you're my best friend?

LIAM. I just thought . . .

ORLA. You haven't said two words to me all year.

LIAM (*shrugs*). I thought people have been giving you the
silent treatment long enough.

ORLA. I don't need your charity, Liam. If the class want to
treat me like a leper, let them. I feel perfectly justified in
what I did.

LIAM. Whatever, Orla, it's in the past now.

ORLA. Not that I give a damn but it probably never occurred
to them there was another side to the story.

LIAM (*tired*). You're right, Orla, it really doesn't matter.

ORLA (*ignores him*). Firstly, the timetable for the sound room
was completely unfair to me. My music had to be edited
before I started shooting. How else could I choreograph
the camera for Broken Doll's dance? It was absolutely vital
I had access to the Pro-Tools before this weekend.

LIAM. Yeah, okay, so the timetable was unfair.

ORLA. But you don't understand, Liam. It was purely out of
spite Nicole took that slot. And she was only messing about
in the sound room.

LIAM. But you never even asked her to swap with you. You could've at least talked to her?

ORLA. She'd never swap with me! I was outside the TV studio at Easter and I overheard her tell Joe she thought I was a lesbian.

ORLA *waits for a response.* LIAM *says nothing.*

I'm not!

LIAM. So . . . ?

ORLA (*shrugs*). She's a bitch.

LIAM. Still, Orla, you don't tell someone their mother's been taken to hospital coz you need to use their computer.

ORLA. But think of the relief when she found out her mother was fine.

LIAM. Did you even know Nicole's mum had cancer?

ORLA. Of course I did! It wouldn't have worked otherwise.

LIAM. You can't do things like that, Orla. Nicole was really freaked out.

ORLA. I didn't know you still cared about her.

LIAM. I just don't get how can you behave like that and think you'll get away with it.

LIAM *goes back to the sofa, to get away from* ORLA.

ORLA. Why did Nicole break up with you?

LIAM. I don't want to talk about it.

ORLA. Maybe you should, Liam? Bring it to the surface rather than keeping it inside? It'll only fester and coalesce into a little black rock of bitter acrimony.

LIAM. Look, Orla, I appreciate your concern but can we just drop it?

ORLA. No, no, you misunderstand, Liam. I'm not concerned, I'm only thinking that the pain could be useful now . . . For your performance.

LIAM (*shakes his head in disbelief*). I can't believe you cried at *E.T.*

ORLA. I did not cry at *E.T.*

LIAM. Orla, there's no shame in admitting it. So you cried at a movie; welcome to the human race.

ORLA. You're delusional.

LIAM. I saw you with my own eyes.

ORLA. I've never cried at a movie in my life!

LIAM *nods.* ORLA *saunters over to the butterfly jar.*

LIAM. I'm not killing it.

ORLA *turns on her heel and saunters back to the camera.*

ORLA. Perhaps it would help you if I show you an example of what I'm after? There's a Maya Derren short that's simply superb.

ORLA *goes over to the pile of videotapes by the wall.*

LIAM (*something occurs to him*). Orla? Earlier when you said I won't tell them if you don't, what did you mean by that?

ORLA. I won't tell anyone in the class that you're acting in my film. So if you don't tell them, your precious reputation among the herd will be more than safe.

LIAM. You didn't tell anyone I was going to help you?

ORLA. No.

LIAM. No one knows I'm here?

ORLA *stares at* LIAM.

ORLA. What?

LIAM. Huh?

ORLA. You look like you've seen a ghost.

LIAM. I have to make a call.

ORLA (*irritated*). Liam, we're in the middle of a scene.

GERARD *enters, carrying a DVD player in its box.*

GERARD. Knock, knock!

ORLA (*surprised*). What are you doing here?

GERARD. I have a little something for you.

LIAM (*to* ORLA). I'll be back in a minute.

> LIAM *goes into the kitchen, takes out his mobile phone and is about to dial when he reconsiders and puts it down.*

ORLA (*to* GERARD). We're in the middle of filming.

GERARD. I didn't ring the bell . . .

> *In the kitchen,* LIAM *sits at the table and puts his head in his hands. He deliberates whether or not to make a phone call but eventually decides not to.* GERARD *puts the box down.*

ORLA. What's that?

GERARD. A DVD player.

ORLA. What's it for?

GERARD. Have you not heard, Orla? There are these shiny little discs, exactly like CDs only they –

ORLA (*interrupts*). I mean what are you doing with it?

GERARD. It's for you, Orla. It's a present.

ORLA (*laughs nervously*). Sorry?

> GERARD *sits on the sofa.* ORLA *notices the script on the sofa. She quickly takes it and stuffs it in her pocket.* GERARD *opens up the DVD box.*

GERARD. It's a top-of-the-range model. Simply plug a lead into the TV and you're away in a hack. It won't take you long to set up at all.

ORLA. Why did you buy it?

GERARD. Does a father need a reason to buy his daughter a present?

ORLA. No, Dad, but I . . . I don't want it.

GERARD. Why ever not?

ORLA. I'm sorry but we need to get back to work. We're in the middle of a vital –

GERARD. What did you do with your hair?

ORLA (*touches her hair*). What?

GERARD. A new haircut, is it?

ORLA (*surprised*). You're the first person to notice.

GERARD (*nods*). It's a haircut alright. (*He points at the DVD player.*) Why don't you want it? You've been talking about getting one for ages.

ORLA. I know, but –

GERARD. How many times have I heard you complain about videos not being in widescreen?

ORLA. I know, Dad.

GERARD. Now we can watch DVDs instead. Isn't that much better?

ORLA *says nothing but then sits beside him.*

ORLA. Dad, please. I already explained. I only have the rest of the weekend to shoot and edit a whole ten-minute film. If it's not finished by Monday then I won't graduate and I won't have a showreel.

GERARD *gets up and examines the dollhouse.*

GERARD. Is this a prop? It's a bit shabby-looking, isn't it?

ORLA. It's supposed to be like that.

GERARD. You're going for a gritty texture to the film? A kind of cheapness? (*Nods.*) Interesting choice.

ORLA. This film will open up a whole new world to me; film festivals, arts funding, maybe even scholarships? It's the beginning of my career as an artist, so it's very important I get it exactly right.

GERARD. Who's that in the kitchen? A replacement for the creep who dropped out?

ORLA. Yes, he's from my class.

GERARD (*surprised*). Really? Someone from your class? A Gaahead or a bimbo?

ORLA (*shrugs*). If I had any other options, I would have taken them.

GERARD. Who is he?

ORLA. Liam Duffy.

GERARD. Name rings a bell.

ORLA. He was the one who stole the trophy for cleanest college, dragged it around on the back of a moped and then put it back in its display case.

GERARD (*remembering*). Oh yes . . . I thought he was expelled.

ORLA. He was going to be but the class protested so the board reconsidered.

GERARD. Typical. And does he like you?

ORLA. Dad, don't be silly.

GERARD. But I'm glad your film's going well. That makes me happy. Glad to be happy . . . and happy to be glad . . . There's a spare Scart lead in my room . . .

GERARD *looks at* ORLA *for a response. She says nothing. A beat.*

It won't take you a minute.

ORLA. I don't want it.

GERARD. What?

ORLA (*nods at the DVD player*). That.

GERARD. Why not?

ORLA *gets up and walks away from him.*

ORLA. No reason.

GERARD. I don't understand.

ORLA. There's nothing to understand.

GERARD. But what's the reason?

ORLA (*shrugs*). No reason.

GERARD. Simply pure irrationality, is it?

ORLA (*thinks, then*). Yes.

GERARD (*blankly*). I have no response to that.

*A beat.*

ORLA. We absolutely have to get back to work now. So I'll see you on Monday, okay?

GERARD *sits down and looks at the DVD player.*

GERARD. The shop assistant in Dixons was one of my pupils, isn't that a coincidence? Last week I caught him chewing gum and made him swallow it. So when he saw me today I bet he was planning revenge . . . Either that or he's a patronising eejit to everyone. He assumed I knew nothing about technology and tried to foist the most expensive one on me. That's all they care about these days; money . . . And sex. Give them a copy of Shakespeare's *Complete Works* and they'd only try sell it on eBay . . . or have sex with it, am I right?

ORLA (*quietly*). Dad, you promised me these few days.

GERARD (*irritated*). Now don't start, Orla! A father does something nice for his child and she bites the head off him like a vicious black widow spider!

GERARD *angrily paces.*

ORLA. I'm not biting the head off you.

GERARD. I never said you were. I'm talking about the black widow spider. It's a deadly predator in Central Asia . . . Orla, why is everything such hard work with you these days? The last year all we ever do is end up bickering . . .

And you always seem to eat in college these days, never home for dinner. You used to love my cooking.

ORLA. It seems strange, that's all.

GERARD. What?

ORLA. Why are you buying me such a big present when I'm in the middle of shooting? All my concentration is on this film. I don't have the mental space to facilitate this right now.

GERARD. It's times like these I wish your mother was still with us. She'd understand what you're on about.

ORLA. If I hook it up now, will you go back to Carmel's after?

GERARD. Of course I will, Orla. Have a look in the box of wires and things under my bed. I'm sure there's a Scart lead there.

ORLA *exits.* GERARD *lifts up the DVD player and looks at it. A moment later,* LIAM *enters from the kitchen.*

LIAM. Hi there. Where's Orla?

GERARD (*not looking at him*). Gone on an errand.

LIAM. Oh . . . Who are you?

GERARD (*re: DVD player*). Why didn't she want this?

LIAM. What?

GERARD. Wouldn't you be happy if you got this as a present? I know she doesn't want me here but I only wanted to do something nice for her.

LIAM. Oh. Are you the actor who dropped out?

GERARD (*hesitates, then*). That's right . . .

LIAM. God, you really dodged a bomb on this one.

GERARD. Tell me, does Orla ever talk about her plans after graduation?

LIAM. We're not that close.

GERARD. Does she ever talk about moving out of home? About getting her own place?

LIAM. No.

GERARD. What about her father? What does she say about him?

LIAM. She's never mentioned him to me. But really we're not pals. We don't hang out.

GERARD. Why has she been so tetchy and secretive lately? Is it because she's moving out? Is that her big secret? And she doesn't want to be lugging a bulky DVD player around with her?

LIAM (*shrugs*). Don't look at me.

GERARD. What did you mean I dodged a bomb on this one?

*LIAM sits on the sofa and eats the rest of his biscuit, catching the crumbs in his other hand.*

LIAM. Man, you've no idea the crap I've put up with over the last few days. All for the sake of art with a capital A, as if that's some great gift to humanity. Thank God this is the last day.

GERARD. Art is very important.

LIAM. Important to pretentious wankers who want to lord it over everyone else.

*LIAM finishes his biscuit and looks at his handful of crumbs. He rubs them into the white shirt.*

And you must be what? At least twenty years older than me? How can I be playing the same character as you? (*Remembers.*) Oh yeah, I'm not a character, I'm a construct . . . You've read the script, could you make any sense of it?

GERARD. I haven't read it. Orla never shows me her work until it's complete.

LIAM. Have you seen her other movies?

GERARD. Yes.

LIAM. And what did you think?

GERARD. I think Orla's a singular talent whose art is exciting and different.

LIAM. Really?

GERARD (*shrugs*). No, I didn't understand them at all . . . but they're important to Orla so I'll support her in any way that I can.

LIAM (*confused*). Hang on, how were you supposed to act in her movie without reading the script?

GERARD (*pauses and looks at* LIAM). Is it any wonder I dropped out?

LIAM *nods and looks down at the DVD player.*

LIAM. I can't believe you bought her a DVD player. It's not like you didn't have a good enough reason to drop out. You really didn't have to do it, y'know?

GERARD (*suspicious*). You'd like that, would you?

LIAM. What?

GERARD *walks over to* LIAM.

GERARD. If I wasn't here. If it was only you and Orla?

LIAM. What d'you mean?

GERARD. You like her, do you? Hoping to make a beeline into her pants?

LIAM (*appalled*). What?! Jesus, no!

GERARD. Why are you here? Is she paying you?

LIAM. No, I'm . . . it's complicated. It's because of my ex-girlfriend Nicole . . . (*Something suddenly occurs to him.*) Actually . . . I know I don't know you but can I ask you a favour?

GERARD. What is it?

LIAM. Well, there's this girl Nicole. She's my ex-girlfriend and I'm trying to get back with her so if –

GERARD. Why did she break up with you?

LIAM. She said I only cared about myself.

GERARD. The motto of your generation, I believe.

LIAM. The thing is, nobody knows I'm working on Orla's movie. And it's Nicole's birthday today. So what I need you to do is ring Nicole, pretending to be someone else who's looking for me. But the real purpose of the call is to actually let her know that I'm helping Orla. Y'know, you could say something like you only just remembered where I was? You're an actor, you can improvise. So when Nicole finds that out . . . she'll ring me.

GERARD. I don't understand.

LIAM. Which bit?

GERARD. All of it. Ring her yourself.

LIAM. I can't just ring her.

GERARD. Why?

LIAM. I can't go crawling back to her after being dumped. There's no way she'd take me back. I have to wait for her to ring me but she won't do that unless she knows I'm here helping Orla . . . I know it sounds nuts but it's really not.

GERARD. Why would the fact you're helping Orla make Nicole ring you?

LIAM. Because Nicole hates Orla.

GERARD. Excuse me?

LIAM. And it's like, the idea I'd work on Orla's movie rather than be around for her birthday will piss her off so much, she'll have no choice but to ring me. And then when she rings I can explain to her that I don't only care about myself.

GERARD. Why would she hate Orla?

LIAM (*shrugs*). Oh, y'know . . .

GERARD (*offended*). I do not know . . . Simply because she doesn't follow the sheep watching *Big Brother* and smoking crack, the herd cuts her off! Is that it?

LIAM. Hey, Orla doesn't care about anyone else in the class, why should we care about her?

GERARD. Every artistic genius was misunderstood in their own lifetime . . . Not that Orla's a genius, but you know what I mean.

LIAM. Anyway, will you ring Nicole for me then?

GERARD *sits on the sofa.*

GERARD. Why on earth would I help you do that? You only want to make her jealous. You want to make her think you and Orla are an item.

LIAM *stares at* GERARD. *A beat.* LIAM *bursts out laughing.*

What's so funny?

LIAM. Nothing, nothing. Look, I'm not trying to make Nicole jealous. I want to get back with her, that's all.

GERARD. You only want to make yourself feel better.

LIAM. No, you don't understand. This will help me get her back.

GERARD. You don't care about her at all!

LIAM *sits down beside* GERARD.

LIAM. No, I do! It's like, y'know the way you go through life with a constant niggling feeling of dissatisfaction? Even when things are grand, there's this vague sense that there's more out there? That there's something better? That somehow you could be living the movie version of your life where you say witty things and girls think you're sexy? And you don't stand in the kitchen for hours trying to decide what to have for breakfast? Well, that's how Nicole makes me feel. Like my life is a movie.

GERARD. Is Nicole actually a girl? Or is it your pet name for cocaine?

LIAM. How can I make you understand?

GERARD. I understand.

LIAM. If you understood, we wouldn't still be talking. You'd be ringing her. Please, she's the only thing in my life that's worth a damn.

GERARD. You're barely out of your teens. How can any girl be so important?

LIAM. Look, let me show you what she's like. I have a video of her.

*LIAM gets a video from his bag and puts it into the video player. He presses play and they watch it. Sounds of babies crying, atonal music and a self-important monologue can be heard.*

That's Nicole there. Now can you tell me she's not the most beautiful thing you've ever seen?

GERARD. She is pretty.

LIAM. And she doesn't care about making a fool of herself. How rare is that in a stunner?

*They watch some more in silence.*

GERARD. What is this video?

LIAM. There was a free afternoon last week so Nicole and some of the class got Orla's script and we made a spoof of it.

GERARD. Excuse me?

LIAM. We were really bored.

GERARD. The class made a parody of Orla's script? But you showed it to her afterward? It was a joke?

LIAM. No, of course not.

VOICE ON TV (*in mock serious tones*). Behind a locked door, her heart is no more worn out . . . By strife, her taciturn scream, lost in the night . . . no more.

GERARD. This is appalling.

LIAM. I know, try saying it on camera!

GERARD (*staring at the TV*). Is this what Orla wants? To be a part of this idiotic rabble? Is this why she wants to abandon me? (*Looks at* LIAM.) Everything I've done for her and now she throws it back in my face.

LIAM (*confused*). What? Did you spend a lot of time rehearsing or something?

GERARD. It wasn't just time. It was love.

LIAM (*shocked*). Love?

GERARD. Yes, love. What am I going to do?

LIAM. You love Orla?

GERARD. Of course I love her.

LIAM (*confused*). Does she know?

GERARD. I try to tell her, I try to show her but she doesn't want to hear.

LIAM. And . . . what about your wife?

GERARD *stares at* LIAM. *A beat.*

GERARD. My wife is dead.

LIAM (*mortified*). Oh God! I'm so sorry. I . . . I didn't know.

GERARD. How would you have known?

LIAM. That's terrible, I . . . Wait, are you saying that you called in here to give Orla a DVD player even though your wife just died in childbirth . . . (*Incredulous.*) And Orla wouldn't forgive you?

GERARD. What in the name of God are you on about? I'm Orla's father.

LIAM (*horrified*). I thought you were that actor.

GERARD (*waves his hand dismissively*). That was a lie.

LIAM. Jesus! (*Quickly turns off TV.*) We were just messing about. Really, it was just for a laugh.

GERARD (*realising*). They'll all laugh at her, won't they? At the graduate screening. The first public screening of her work and she'll be greeted with howls of laughter . . .

LIAM. It was just a joke. It doesn't mean anything.

GERARD. What are you saying? It means everything to her! It's Orla's whole world. That's all she ever does. All she ever talks about. And now she'll be ripped to shreds like a pine marten in a den of panthers.

*They sit in silence for a few moments.*

LIAM. Do panthers live in dens?

GERARD. That is absolutely irrelevant! . . . What am I going to do about her film?

LIAM. Maybe you could have a talk with her. I don't mean tell her about it, but . . . I don't know . . .

GERARD (*thinking*). No, no, you're right. It's not too late. You're saying I should stop her finishing the film?

LIAM. What?! No, that's not what I'm saying at all!

GERARD. I could say something so that she'll let me stay . . . What if I was sick or something? Dying, even.

LIAM (*appalled*). What?

GERARD. No? Too much?

LIAM. You can't tell her that!

GERARD. How can I be thinking this? But what kind of a father sits back and lets his only daughter be humiliated? Whatever my personal feelings or whatever the consequences, at the end of the day I'm her father and I have to protect her. Then the question becomes, not how can I do this but, how can I not? This film must not be made and that video must not be seen . . . And the pine marten might yet survive. Am I right?

*A beat.*

LIAM. So, anyway . . . will you ring Nicole for me?

ORLA *enters.*

ORLA. There was no Scart lead in that box.

GERARD. I must have been mistaken. Maybe I gave it to Carmel when she got her new TV?

ORLA. Dad, I'll go and buy a lead on Monday and connect it then, okay?

GERARD. Okay, Orla . . .

ORLA. I better get back to work. Liam's very dedicated to his craft . . . He'll get edgy if we don't get shooting soon, isn't that right, Liam?

LIAM (*flustered*). Eh, yeah, sure . . . I have to use the toilet.

LIAM *hurriedly exits.*

ORLA. Auntie Carmel will be wondering where you are.

GERARD. I have all my books here and the television.

ORLA. Carmel has a television.

GERARD. Yes, but she doesn't have my books.

ORLA. Take some with you.

GERARD. Orla, she hates me. She thinks I'm a bore and an intellectual snob.

ORLA. That's not true, Dad.

GERARD *gets up and walks over to the fish tank. He taps the glass.*

GERARD. I've spent the last four days listening to her complain about her sciatica and her rheumatism and the poisonous spider eggs nestled in her pancreas! Why can't I stay here?

ORLA. You could give someone a call. Go out for dinner with them.

GERARD. Who?

ORLA. I don't know. Someone from school?

GERARD. They don't like me either.

ORLA. Go to the cinema. Or a play.

GERARD. On my own?

ORLA (*starting to panic*). But Dad, you promised. I told you how important this film is to me.

*At the mention of film, something suddenly occurs to GERARD. He goes back to the TV.*

GERARD. Orla, you're being irrational. It won't make the slightest difference if I stay here.

ORLA (*pleading*). No, Dad, it has to be only me and Liam this weekend.

GERARD. Orla, it is *my* house.

ORLA. I asked you for this months ago and you said it was no problem.

GERARD. Did I say that? Doesn't sound like me.

ORLA. You did.

GERARD. I'll stay in my room and you won't hear a peep. You won't hear a pip.

ORLA. Dad, please, I never ask you for any time to myself. All I'm asking for is this weekend.

GERARD. What would your mother say if she saw you treating me like this? She'd be horrified, Orla. Horrified! Kicking me out of our home to spend the weekend with someone who doesn't like me. Do you think Mum would do that if she was still with us? Do you think she'd be proud of you right now?

ORLA *walks away from him, saying nothing.* GERARD *sees his chance and discretely ejects the tape from the video player. He looks around and then sticks it under the coffee table. He turns back to* ORLA.

Well, do you?

ORLA (*quietly*). No.

GERARD. No . . . The only way we have of honouring her memory is to do what she would want. Am I right?

ORLA *says nothing.*

Now, I'll go to my room and read my books. You make your film and the next time you see me, it'll be Monday morning . . . You won't even hear a puh!

GERARD *exits.* ORLA, *seething with frustration, goes to the shelf of videos and makes herself busy looking for a particular one. She finds it and pulls it out of a stack but the rest of the tapes fall to the ground with a clatter. ORLA, immobilised with frustration, stares at the mess. She then takes a deep breath, regains her composure and puts the video into the player. She goes to the hall.*

ORLA (*loud*). Liam?

*A few moments later, LIAM enters.*

LIAM. Is, eh . . . everything okay?

ORLA. Fine.

ORLA *throws the white shirt to* LIAM *and goes to the camera.* LIAM *puts the shirt on and stands at the dollhouse.* ORLA *turns off the lights* (*leaving* LIAM *in a spotlight*) *and goes behind the camera.*

Are you ready to go again?

LIAM. Oh. Okay. Will I slate it?

ORLA. Yes.

LIAM *prepares the clapperboard then holds it up before the camera.*

Rolling.

LIAM. Slate 40, take 32.

ORLA. Settle and . . . action.

LIAM.
   She has no future, no chance . . .
   To soar, her wings will become dust . . .
   Behind a locked door, her heart is no more lacerated –

ORLA. You're trying to sabotage my film, aren't you?

LIAM. Huh?

ORLA. This is merely a sardonic joke to you.

LIAM (*shocked*). What?

ORLA *turns on the lights.*

ORLA. I get it now, Liam. You're failing the year, so you want me to fail as well?

LIAM. Orla, don't be ridiculous.

ORLA. Why are you being so shit with this speech? Do you know what passion is, Liam? Do you understand the concept? Maybe I have a dictionary around here somewhere.

LIAM (*sighs*). Y'know, Orla, you shouldn't get too obsessed with your movie . . . and y'know, whatever reaction it gets . . .

ORLA. I'm not obsessed, I'm . . . committed.

LIAM. I know, I'm just saying there's more to life than art, y'know?

ORLA. So, I have no life. Is that what you're trying to say!?

LIAM (*under his breath*). No, that's what I'm trying *not* to say.

ORLA. I have a very full life, thank you very much!

LIAM. You never come to Bakers with us at the weekends.

ORLA. I write at the weekends. Besides, getting drunk and swapping fart jokes with a bunch of talking Nike logos is not high on my to-do list!

LIAM. You never even came to the Christmas social.

ORLA. Actually, I was going to but . . . Why are we even talking about this?

LIAM (*shrugs*). I don't know.

LIAM *sees the mess of videotapes on the ground.*

What happened over there?

ORLA. Nothing.

LIAM. Are you sure you're okay?

ORLA. Yes, Liam.

*A beat.*

LIAM. Well, can I ask you for a favour?

ORLA. What?

LIAM. Could you ring Nicole and ask her for my mobile number? And could you explain I'm working on your film this weekend and I've gone out of my way to help you. Maybe I've gone out to Bray to pick up some equipment for you but now you have to contact me coz you also need me to get a diopter, or something. You got that?

ORLA (*completely baffled*). Why do you want me to do that?

LIAM. Because I'm trying to get back . . . (*Stops himself.*) I mean, I want to . . . get back at her.

ORLA. What?

LIAM (*lying*). I want revenge.

ORLA. For who?

LIAM. Me . . . eh, both of us.

ORLA. What?

LIAM *walks over to* ORLA.

LIAM. It's revenge for me coz she dumped me for being selfish, but this shows I'm not selfish coz I'm helping you with your film. And it's revenge for you because . . . she said you were gay.

ORLA. I don't care about that any more.

LIAM. Please, Orla? It'd mean a lot to me.

ORLA. I didn't know you were the vengeful type.

LIAM. Yeah, well.

ORLA. If anything, I would've thought you missed her.

LIAM. Why would I miss her?

ORLA. I don't know.

LIAM. Having to wait hours for her to put on her make-up and then she looks exactly the same as before? Freezing up whenever I went to kiss her in public?

ORLA. Liam, I'm not in the mood.

LIAM. You were right. She's a bitch.

ORLA. You agreed to help me so can we focus on the film? I have that Maya Derren short I was telling you about. Hopefully it'll give you a sense of what I'm after.

ORLA *turns on the TV.* LIAM, *alarmed, goes over to her.*

LIAM *(flustered)*. Orla, I don't think that'd help, really!

ORLA. It has exactly the right mood of jubilant ferocity I'm after.

LIAM. Oh sure! Jubilant ferocity, I get it now.

ORLA. Are you mocking me?

LIAM. No! I mean it. I think I know what you want now. Let's shoot it while it's still in my head.

ORLA. Have you seen the remote anywhere?

ORLA *looks around for the remote control.* LIAM *tries to think of something to say. He stands in front of the TV.*

LIAM. Orla, what's the story with you and your dad?

ORLA. There's no story.

LIAM *touches her arm.*

LIAM. Orla . . .

ORLA *(nervous)*. What?

ORLA *hesitates but then walks over to the dollhouse.* LIAM, *relieved, turns off the TV.* ORLA *rearranges the dollhouse furniture.* LIAM *looks at her, genuinely concerned.*

LIAM. Y'know, Orla, sometimes it is good to talk about things. You don't have to keep it all inside . . . I mean, if you don't want to.

ORLA. It's fine, Liam. Dad's a bit of a handful sometimes, that's all.

LIAM. What d'you mean?

ORLA. He gets . . . anxious. It's funny. That's why I never made it to the Christmas social. (*Chuckles.*) Dad accidentally

locked himself in the bathroom and we spent hours trying
to open the door. Eventually he got it open but by that time
it was too late to go out.

LIAM. How do you accidentally lock yourself in a bathroom?

ORLA. The lock got jammed or something. (*Shrugs.*) I don't
know.

LIAM. And has it ever jammed since then?

ORLA (*suddenly irritated*). What's your point?

LIAM (*embarrassed*). I don't know. It's none of my business.

ORLA *goes back to the camera.*

ORLA. Maybe we should do the apple shots next. I haven't
actually tried getting the worm to wriggle on cue but I have
a hairdryer on standby . . .

LIAM. So, will you ring Nicole for me?

ORLA. Do I look like your personal secretary?

LIAM. Please, Orla. It'll only take a second.

ORLA. I don't want to hear that pudenda-head's voice. What
difference will it make if I ring her?

LIAM. It'll make a difference to me.

ORLA. Jesus, Liam, get over it.

LIAM. Don't you think I want to, Orla? I watched *Disclosure*
last weekend and there was shagging tears in my eyes by
the end of it. I was never like that before I met her.

ORLA. Watched what?

LIAM. *Disclosure*. With Michael Douglas?

ORLA. Have I seen it? What's it about?

LIAM (*sighs*). Michael Douglas works in this big computer
company and wants to get a promotion but then Demi
Moore is made his new boss and sexually harasses him.
And when he goes to make a complaint, she's already said
that he sexually harassed her.

ORLA (*trying to remember*). What happens then?

LIAM (*breaking down throughout*). Well, it turns out it was all a plan to get Michael Douglas fired and he finds out because someone sends him these anonymous e-mails so in the end he has to go into virtual reality and fight this robot Demi Moore. And then in the end they announce who got the promotion and it turns out to be this woman in her 60s who's been with the company the longest and turns out it was her who sent the e-mails and she's actually the person who deserved the promotion all along and Michael Douglas starts clapping and Jesus Christ, I'm getting fucking teary-eyed again!

ORLA. Sounds like shit.

LIAM *wipes his eyes.*

LIAM. It is! That's what I'm saying! So, please, Orla, do this one thing for me and ring Nicole!

ORLA. Jesus, Liam, what's wrong with you?

LIAM. I don't know! I don't know what the fuck is wrong with me. So come on, Orla, I'm begging you.

*A beat.*

ORLA. Okay, Liam. On one condition.

LIAM. What?

ORLA *holds up the butterfly jar.*

ORLA. You kill the butterfly.

*A beat.*

LIAM. Okay.

ORLA. What's her number?

LIAM *scribbles the phone number on a script and hands it to* ORLA.

Fine. I'll do it now and then we get back to filming, okay? Do you want to come and listen?

LIAM (*something occurs to him*). Eh . . . no. No, you go ahead.

ORLA *goes into the kitchen.* LIAM *makes sure she's gone, then goes to the video player, ejects the tape and stuffs it down the back of the sofa. Tired, he sits down and sighs.*

*Meanwhile, in the kitchen,* ORLA *rings Nicole.*

ORLA. Hi, is this Nicole? Hello, it's Orla . . . (*Annoyed.*) Orla from your class. I was wondering if you had Liam's phone number? Only he's working on my film this weekend and he's gone out to Bray to . . . No, I'm not joking. He's acting in it . . . Why is that so hard to believe? . . . How can I prove it? I told you he's not here . . . Now, why on earth would I make up such a thing? . . . Fine, you conceited little pillowcase, you want proof? I was talking to Liam yesterday, and he said the vast amounts of make-up you wear don't make any difference to your ugly mug. And he thinks you're a frigid bitch because you never kissed him in public. So how else would I know about that? . . . Well, there you go. Now if you'll excuse me, I have to get back to my movie.

ORLA *hangs up.*

(*To herself.*) I mean film.

*Lights go down.*

## ACT TWO

*Saturday night. The living room is bare except for the dollhouse, fish tank and the DVD player on the ground; all the film equipment is packed away in cases, the clapperboard is on top of them. In the kitchen, the white shirt is hanging on the back of a chair.* GERARD *enters.*

GERARD. Orla?

> GERARD *looks around and sees there's no one in. He looks at the equipment, picks up the clapperboard and exits.*
>
> *A few moments later,* ORLA *enters. She goes into the kitchen and examines the white shirt, carefully holding it up to the light.*
>
> *Meanwhile,* GERARD *enters again without the clapperboard. He doesn't notice* ORLA *in the kitchen. He tries to open the heavy-duty camera case.* ORLA *walks into the living-room.*

ORLA. Dad?

GERARD (*startled*). Nothing.

ORLA. What are you doing?

GERARD (*flustered*). I wasn't doing anything.

ORLA. Why were you at the camera?

GERARD. I wasn't *at* it. What's that supposed to mean? I only wanted to check it was okay.

ORLA. Why?

GERARD (*sighs, then with infinite patience*). I was lying on my bed wracked with guilt about what happened at dinner, so I said I'd come down and check with Orla that everything was alright. But then you weren't here so I was going to check it myself. That's not a crime, is it?

ORLA. Dad . . . is there something you want to tell me?

GERARD. What do you mean?

ORLA. You know the camera's fine. You saw me catch it.

GERARD. I'm no expert on digital cameras! As far as I know, catching it like that may have jostled the inner workings and done serious damage. I was concerned.

ORLA. Dad, why are you here?

GERARD. Orla, I live here.

ORLA. Why did you knock the camera over earlier and why were you trying to get at it now?

GERARD (*suddenly outraged*). Orla! What are you implying? I told you it was an accident, I didn't even see the camera!

ORLA. Dad, I'm not picking a fight. I'm only asking why you wouldn't stay at Carmel's today.

GERARD. Is that what you wore out?

ORLA. Sorry?

GERARD. Traipsing around on a Saturday night without a jacket? You'll catch your death of cold, Orla, I'm telling you.

ORLA. I was only down the road.

GERARD. If you want to catch pneumonia and join your mother in an early grave, don't let me stop you.

ORLA. If it was cold, I would've worn a jacket.

GERARD. How would you clean curry out of a dollhouse? Answer me that?

ORLA. Well, you –

GERARD (*holds up a hand*). Wait, I'm making a speech . . . It's not easy juggling a plate of curry in one hand and a glass of Chardonnay in the other. I was so intent on saving the dollhouse that I involuntarily nudged the camera with my elbow, it's as simple as that.

ORLA (*quietly*). You pushed it with your hand. I saw –

GERARD (*interrupts*). So you're not going to put on a jacket?

ORLA. What?

GERARD. At least warm yourself up before you catch a chill.

ORLA. But it's not only the camera. Was it really necessary to make a Thai green curry from scratch for dinner? And what about the Maya Derren tape that mysteriously vanished from the video?

GERARD. Orla, what has gotten into you? What are you saying?

ORLA. I'm not accusing you, Dad. I just want to know how, when I told you to be extra, extra careful around Liam's white shirt, you somehow managed to spill wine all down the front of it.

GERARD *walks into the kitchen towards the shirt.*

GERARD. Now, Orla. You can barely see the stain!

ORLA *panics and runs in after him.* GERARD *goes to pick it up.*

ORLA (*fearful*). Will you not touch it, Dad? Please!?

GERARD *gives* ORLA *a look.*

GERARD. Have you been drinking?

ORLA (*defensive*). I had a few.

GERARD. Ah, it all becomes clear! Do you even realise how paranoid you're being right now? Where were you?

ORLA. Liam and I went to McSorley's.

GERARD. Tell me, Orla, since when is getting intoxicated a necessary part of the cinematic process?

ORLA *turns around and walks back into the living room.* GERARD *follows.*

ORLA. I had no choice. Liam insisted. He needed Dutch courage to shoot the final scene.

GERARD. Orla, you don't have to explain yourself. You're free to do whatever you want.

ORLA. He'll be back any minute now and then we're going to start shooting again. So if you could finish what you're doing and go upstairs, I'd very much appreciate it. (*Notices the clapperboard is gone.*) Where's the clapperboard? I left it right here.

GERARD. Orla, what happened to your lip?

ORLA (*embarrassed*). Nothing.

GERARD. Did you burn it? Let me see.

GERARD *holds her head up to the light.*

ORLA. It's nothing. I burnt it on a glass.

GERARD. You have to put some cream on it or it'll swell up.

ORLA. It's fine.

GERARD. What were you doing?

ORLA. Liam was teaching me a trick.

GERARD. What trick?

ORLA (*embarrassed*). How to drink a flaming sambuca.

GERARD. And how was your lip burnt?

ORLA. He's a shit teacher.

GERARD. It's becoming increasingly apparent how much you didn't want to be there.

ORLA. Dad, I'm twenty-two. What's wrong with going for a couple of drinks with a friend? And no, at first I didn't want to be there. But to tell you the truth, after a while, I actually started to have a good time. It felt good to simply sit and chat with someone my own age for a change. Every night, all I do is stay in and watch films with you. Is it too much –

GERARD. Your mother would want you to keep me company, Orla.

ORLA. But wouldn't Mum want me to have friends? To go out once in a while and –

GERARD. I'm dying.

ORLA. Sorry?

GERARD. I think I'm dying.

ORLA. What? How are you dying?

GERARD. I have cancer.

ORLA (*shocked*). What?

GERARD. Now, I may not be dying. It could be benign. The doctor said he'd ring me today to give me the news. Whether it's benign or . . . the other one. I'm still waiting for the call.

ORLA. But it's half eleven . . . And it's Saturday.

GERARD. Those doctors are worked to the bone.

ORLA (*laughs nervously*). Dad, why are you saying this?

GERARD. I thought you'd want to know.

ORLA. Is . . . is this really the truth, Dad? Really?

GERARD. Yes, Orla! Of course it is.

ORLA *says nothing.* GERARD *stares at her.*

You don't believe me, do you?

ORLA (*shrugs*). I don't know, maybe, sure.

GERARD (*serious*). I found a lump so I went to the doctor and he said he'd ring me today to let me know but he thought it was probably cancer.

ORLA. So why didn't you mention this before?

GERARD. You've been so busy with your film, Orla, and it might still be nothing. And so here I am, waiting for what is, without fear of exaggeration, the single most important phone call I will ever receive . . . And I don't want to be alone when I answer it. I wanted to be with you when I found out, Orla. That's why I didn't stay at Carmel's today.

*A beat.*

ORLA. Is this because I didn't want the DVD player?

GERARD (*infuriated*). Jesus Christ, Orla! Do you think I would make up something like this after what we went through when your mother died? That black hole that nearly swallowed us up, those years of grey, meaningless pain? Do you honestly think I would use that for my own ends? That I would put you through that again?

ORLA, *unsure, looks at* GERARD. *A beat.*

ORLA. You . . . you should have said something.

GERARD. It might still be . . . (*Trails off.*)

ORLA. What?

GERARD. Nothing.

ORLA. No, what?

GERARD. No, it might still be nothing.

ORLA. How do you feel? Maybe you should sit down or something . . . Will I get you . . . anything?

GERARD *sits on the sofa.* ORLA *sits beside him.*

GERARD. Orla, I'm fine. There's no need to make a fuss.

ORLA *feels something press into her back. She reaches around and pulls out the video from the back of the sofa.*

ORLA. Oh.

GERARD. What's that?

ORLA. It's that Maya Derren video . . . How did it get down there? . . . Have you told Carmel?

GERARD. No, no. I'll wait until I know for certain.

ORLA. I think we should tell her. She'd know all about this kind of thing. She'll know what's best.

GERARD. Nonsense, Orla. You have to go and put some cream on that lip.

ORLA. What?

GERARD. Otherwise it'll swell up like a balloon and everyone will think you're Mick Jagger.

*A beat.*

Well, go on then.

ORLA. Okay.

ORLA *hesitates, then exits. She puts the video on top of the TV as she leaves.* GERARD *holds his head in his hands. A few moments later,* LIAM, *a bit drunk, enters.*

LIAM. Hi there. Where's Orla?

GERARD (*angry*). Why? So you can finish the job and set fire to the rest of her face?

LIAM. What?

GERARD. Why not simply douse her in petrol and be done with it! You don't give a damn about her well-being, do you? Don't give a shit? What kind of a person are you!?

LIAM. Jesus, don't blame me! She begged me to show her that trick.

GERARD. Begged you, did she? That's not the way Orla tells it. She said you had her trapped in that pub all night.

LIAM. Okay, it was my idea to go but after one drink, you couldn't move her for love nor money.

GERARD. Is that the truth?

LIAM. Yes.

GERARD (*sighs*). What has happened to us? . . . How did we end up like this?

LIAM (*points to DVD*). Hey, since you're not the actor, why did you bring this over?

GERARD (*waves hand dismissively*). I just needed an excuse to call in.

LIAM. Does Orla cry at movies?

GERARD. No.

LIAM. I mean, has she ever cried at a movie?

GERARD. No.

LIAM. Never?

GERARD. No.

LIAM. But I saw her cry at *E.T.* Why won't she just admit it?

*LIAM shrugs and looks around the room for something.*

GERARD. I've always valued Orla's honesty. Such a rare and admirable quality . . . I remember one Sunday when Orla was sixteen . . . We'd been out to Deansgrange that morning to visit Helen's grave and then spent the afternoon staring blankly at the telly. The world was just an out-of-focus blur back then, no rhyme nor reason to any of it . . . I asked Orla what she wanted for dinner and she had this odd look on her face and then asked me to make something different. Something wild and strange and exotic. So I did . . . And that evening we sat down to our catfish and prune risotto with grilled onion pudding and Orla took one bite, looked at me and said . . . This tastes like feet . . . And we laughed. And suddenly, just a little, the world came back into focus. And I knew we were going to be okay . . . That feels like a long time ago. Now she doesn't care about me any more. Not really . . . All she cares about is her film.

*LIAM stares at GERARD. A beat.*

LIAM. You do know what her movie's about, don't you?

GERARD. What?

LIAM. You.

*A beat.*

GERARD. Repeat that.

LIAM. The movie's about you. At least, that's what Orla said.

GERARD. What? What do you mean?

LIAM (*shrugs*). I think it was only tonight after a few drinks that she realised it herself. She was about to explain it but we got distracted when I eh, accidentally set the table on fire . . . it was only a little fire, just a few flames really . . .

GERARD (*shocked*). How is her film about me?

LIAM. I don't know . . . (*Thinks about it.*) I guess Broken Doll must be Orla and the butterfly represents you. In the movie, she doesn't want it to die and when it does, she's heartbroken.

GERARD. No wonder she didn't want me here this – (*Something occurs to him.*) My God, I've been such a fool! All this time I thought her secretiveness, the arguments, everything, was because she planned to move out . . . but that wasn't it at all. Her secret is that the film is about me. And there I was, prodding and pushing and sticking my nose in. No wonder she's been so cranky. (*Laughs.*) Oh, Gerard Cullen, what an idiot you are! . . . But if she isn't moving out, why didn't she want this? (*Points to DVD.*)

LIAM *spots* GERARD *is sitting on his jacket.*

LIAM. Sorry, can I just . . . ?

LIAM *points at his jacket.*

GERARD. Oh.

GERARD *stands up and hands the jacket to* LIAM. LIAM *takes it but then* GERARD *won't let go of the other end.*

(*Suddenly realising.*) Where are you going?

LIAM. Town.

GERARD. But . . . what about the film?

LIAM. What about it?

GERARD. I thought you needed Dutch courage to do the last shot?

LIAM. No, I needed to get so shit-faced I couldn't remember my own name. But that didn't work and then I wasted the twenty minutes trying to score some weed but no joy. So now I have to go and shagging find her.

GERARD. Who?

LIAM. Nicole.

GERARD. She didn't ring?

LIAM. It just doesn't add up. Orla rang her this afternoon and told her I was here. I know Nicole, she can't ignore anything that gets on her wick . . . How is this not tearing her up inside? I have to find out.

GERARD. But you have to stay and finish the film.

LIAM. I thought you didn't want her to finish it?

GERARD. That was before.

LIAM. Before what?

GERARD. Before I knew it was a tribute to me. All these years, everything I've done for Orla . . . This is her way of thanking me, of showing how much she appreciates our life together . . . You have to finish it.

LIAM *yanks the jacket out of* GERARD*'s hand.*

LIAM. I have to go.

GERARD. Dublin's a big city. How are you going to find her?

LIAM. She always has her birthday in Doyles.

GERARD. You don't get it, do you? Nicole doesn't want you. Not ringing is her way of telling you that the relationship is dead.

LIAM. I don't know that.

GERARD. You have all the proof you need! She didn't ring. She doesn't care. Am I right?

LIAM. No. You're not.

GERARD. It's a perfectly understandable mistake to make. You and this girl got drunk a few times, slept with each other, swapped heart-warming stories about growing up with low IQs . . . Of course you assume you're soul mates but that simply wasn't the case.

LIAM. No, me and Nicole was real. She didn't see me the way everyone else did. I wasn't just a drinking buddy, y'know? She wouldn't even go out with me until I'd written more of my script.

GERARD (*surprised*). Oh.

LIAM. What?

GERARD. You write?

LIAM (*annoyed*). Yeah, it's what I specialised in. Why is that so hard to believe?

GERARD (*shrugs*). You don't look the type.

LIAM (*angry*). Jesus! You take one look at me and assume I'm some loser who's going to spend the rest of his life working in Supermacs, is that it? Is that what you think?

*A beat.*

GERARD. Yes.

LIAM *sits down on the sofa.*

LIAM. See, that's what I'm saying. Nicole didn't see me like that. She read the first ten pages of my graduate script and they made her laugh. She said they were hilarious. Then the next week I tried to kiss her at a social but she was having none of it. Ten more pages, she said, then I'll kiss you. I thought she was taking the piss but she was dead serious. Can you believe that? So I knocked out ten more pages but it's like, I didn't even have to *think* about them. My fingers touched the keyboard and they were off! The next time I looked at the clock it was 5am. I loved that . . . Staying up, on my own, writing till the sun came up . . . I started going out with Nicole after that and all that time, she kept encouraging me to write. So don't tell me that she never really cared about me, okay?

GERARD. Did you finish the script?

LIAM. Nah, I haven't written since she dumped me.

GERARD *sits beside* LIAM.

GERARD. I'm sorry to hear that. What's your script about?

LIAM. I don't want to talk about it.

GERARD. What's it called?

LIAM. Look, forget it. Nicole was wrong, it was probably shit. I should have done camera with the rest of the guys.

GERARD. Don't be ashamed because you want to strive for something more in life. Art is how we grapple with the senseless chaos of existence. Art is always worthwhile. Never forget that.

LIAM. It's called *Goodnight Sweet Prawn*. It's about a prawn fisher who's mistaken for a famous Shakespearean actor and falls in love with a gangster's daughter.

GERARD (*blankly*). I have no response to that.

*A beat.*

LIAM (*gets up to leave*). Say goodbye to Orla for me.

GERARD. And what makes you think Nicole will take you back?

LIAM (*shrugs*). That's how it works in the movies. I run through the rain and get to the airport just in time to stop her leaving. So that's what I'm going to do. There's a happy ending waiting for me out there, I know there is.

GERARD. That's nothing but Hollywood claptrap. The world does not work like that.

LIAM. How do you know?

GERARD *stands up and faces* LIAM.

GERARD. I know because ten years ago, my wife slipped on the wet kitchen floor and cracked her head open on the sideboard. Do you think if I pray hard enough she'll magically reappear in a puff of smoke and a harp glissando?

LIAM. No, I don't but –

GERARD. Or do you think a mature but attractive widow with a sharp and sassy nature will move in next door, who I'll bicker with incessantly for years, until eventually discovering our mutual love for each other?

LIAM. Look, all I'm saying is –

GERARD. Or do you think . . . (*Stops in his tracks.*) I can't think of any other happy endings . . . But they're all equally preposterous and have absolutely nothing to do with real life!

LIAM. But I have a chance with Nicole, I know I do. I can't let it slip through my fingers.

GERARD (*laughs*). Now you even sound like the hero of a corny B-movie!

LIAM. So? What's wrong with that? (*Looks at his watch.*) I have to catch the last bus.

GERARD (*shrugs*). No one's stopping you.

LIAM *puts on his jacket and heads to the door.* GERARD *sits down.*

(*Casually.*) But there's one thing you haven't thought of . . .

LIAM *stops, hesitates, then turns around.*

LIAM. What?

GERARD. What if you're not the hero?

LIAM. What?

GERARD. What if you're actually the bad guy?

LIAM. What d'you mean?

GERARD. You talk about dashing off and winning the girl back like they do in the movies. But it's always the hero who gets the girl. The good, virtuous person who deserves his happy ending.

LIAM. So?

GERARD. So, what have you done that makes you the hero?

LIAM. I . . . okay, so I haven't done anything amazing but I'm not the worst person in the world.

GERARD. The bad guy never thinks of himself as the bad guy, isn't that right?

LIAM. Yeah, but –

GERARD. So you could be bad and not know it.

LIAM. No I know, but –

GERARD. Nicole is a beautiful and funny girl who, no doubt, could have her pick of men. What makes you think you deserve someone like that?

LIAM. Well, because . . .

GERARD. When you look at your life; the drunkenness, the vandalism, the drugs –

LIAM (*unsure*). I'm not that bad.

GERARD. Making fun of people behind their back, lying and using people for your own ends . . . Setting furniture ablaze? Do you really think Nicole deserves to be with someone like that? Am I right?

*A beat.*

LIAM. I don't feel so good.

GERARD. Because you know what will happen if you go and confront Nicole? You'll stagger into the pub and you'll find her in the corner, sitting close to another man, holding his hand, maybe even kissing him. And do you know who that man is? . . . *He's* the hero.

LIAM, *depressed, sits on the sofa again.*

You wanted to know why Nicole never rang. I think you have your answer . . . So you'll stay?

LIAM *takes off his jacket.* ORLA *enters.* GERARD *takes* LIAM's *jacket from him and hangs it up on the coat rack.*

ORLA. How are you, Dad? Do you need anything?

GERARD. A good night's sleep is all I need right now. I'll leave you two in peace to finish your film.

ORLA. Dad.

GERARD. Now, Orla, you're not to worry about me, okay?

ORLA *nods.*

GERARD *exits.* ORLA, *concerned, watches him leave.*

LIAM. Is it okay if I crash here tonight?

ORLA (*troubled*). Sure, if you want.

LIAM. Are you alright? You look a bit . . .

ORLA (*forced smile*). I'm fine . . . too much sambuca, that's all.

LIAM. Ever feel like if you were never born, it wouldn't make any difference?

ORLA. Liam, what's wrong with you?

LIAM (*shakes his head, embarrassed*). Forget it, I'm an idiot.

ORLA. You're the most popular person in the class, Liam.

LIAM. Just coz I can drink the most.

ORLA. Everyone loves you. You're not a loser.

LIAM. I never said I was a loser! What made you say that?

> ORLA, *mortified, doesn't respond.* LIAM *puts his head in his hands. While looking down, he spots the videotape under the coffee-table. He picks it up and puts it on the table.*

> Did Nicole say anything else to you earlier?

ORLA. Liam, don't waste your time thinking about her. She's nothing but a little shit. Shit from a bottom.

LIAM. How did she sound on the phone?

ORLA. I don't know, bland.

LIAM. Was she upset?

ORLA. Liam, relax, you got your own back. She probably burst into tears after I hung up. Isn't that what you wanted?

LIAM. Yeah . . . I just . . . Sometimes I don't get her at all.

ORLA. What's to get? You might as well try to understand a sheet of paper or some belly-button fluff. You should try to take your mind off her. It was so funny when you spilt that flaming sambuca on the table. I couldn't stop laughing.

LIAM (*glum*). Yeah, hilarious.

ORLA *goes to the TV and picks up the tape she left on top of it.*

ORLA. I found that tape I was going to show you. It got down the back of the sofa somehow.

LIAM's *face turns white. He stands up.*

LIAM. Orla. Hang on.

ORLA *puts the tape into the video player.*

Orla, wait.

ORLA (*turns and looks at* LIAM). What?

LIAM. What about the last shot? Don't you want to finish the film? I really feel I'm ready to do it now. But *right* now!

ORLA. Oh. Okay.

LIAM. Quick, go and set up the camera before I chicken out again!

ORLA. Right.

ORLA *goes and sets up the camera.* LIAM *breathes a sigh of relief, quickly ejects the tape in the player, puts it in his bag and then puts in the tape he found under the coffee table. Just as he's finished,* ORLA *turns around.*

LIAM. Actually, do you want to show me this video first?

ORLA. The what?

LIAM (*points at the TV*). The Maya whatever movie. Jubilant ferocity?

*A beat.*

ORLA (*shakes her head*). Forget it, it's not important. Let's just get this done and call it a night.

LIAM *rolls his eyes, after all the trouble he's gone to switch the tapes.*

LIAM. Okay. Whatever . . . (*Looking around him.*) Do you have the script?

ORLA *takes the roof off the dollhouse and gets the script from inside the roof. LIAM takes it from her, staring at her like she's crazy. ORLA catches his look.*

ORLA. What?

LIAM. It's a script, Orla, not the bloody crown jewels.

LIAM *shakes his head in disbelief. ORLA looks troubled. She turns away. Behind her, LIAM looks around for the white shirt. He spots it in the kitchen and goes to get it. ORLA doesn't notice that he's left the room.*

ORLA. You know I was telling you in the pub how I realised my film's about Dad? Well, I never finished telling you . . . I suppose it was the drink tonight that made it suddenly clear to me, what I've been denying for so long . . . My film's about what a horrific, selfish man my dad truly is . . . and tonight I learnt he might actually . . . have cancer. That's why I can't leave the script lying around, Liam . . .

LIAM, *in the kitchen, doesn't hear what ORLA says. He holds the shirt up to the light, looking at the stain, then puts it on. He walks back into the living room, looking down at the stain.*

I have to do everything I can to keep it out of sight.

LIAM (*rubbing the stain*). It'll be fine, Orla. I'll keep it well hidden.

ORLA (*touched, looks at LIAM*). I didn't know you cared.

LIAM. Really, it's not a problem. I'll just hide it with my hands if I have to.

ORLA (*puzzled*). Okay . . .

LIAM. D'you want to do this then?

ORLA *nods. LIAM stands behind the dollhouse, takes the fluttering butterfly out of the jar and holds it in his hands. ORLA turns off the lights (leaving LIAM in a spotlight) and goes behind the camera.*

(*Looks around.*) Where's the clapperboard?

ORLA. Forget it, it's the last shot anyway. Ready?

LIAM *nods.*

Rolling . . . And action.

LIAM.
She has no future, no chance . . .
To soar, her wings will become dust . . .
Behind a locked door, her heart is no more . . .
Worn out by strife. Her taciturn scream . . .
Lost in the night, no more . . .

*He holds up the live butterfly.*

Dreams know nothing . . .
No life . . .

ORLA. Wait!

LIAM. Yeah?

ORLA. I'm not sure.

LIAM. About what?

ORLA. The butterfly.

LIAM. Really? Coz it's funny but that take actually felt . . .
kind of good. Maybe it's just holding it in my hands or
maybe it's the five pints of Heineken but I think I got a flash
of what you're going for.

ORLA. That's good but I don't know.

LIAM. What do you mean?

ORLA. I don't know if . . . you should kill it.

LIAM. I don't mind.

ORLA. It's not that.

LIAM. Coz I think I get it now. I get why you want me to.

ORLA. You do?

LIAM. Yeah, the scene's about the relationship between the
two characters. Broken Doll keeps trying to please Man in
White but really, the relationship's over. He kills the

butterfly to prove this to her. The butterfly represents their
relationship. He has to kill it.

ORLA. Okay, yes, but just use the words. Convey the same
feeling with the words.

LIAM. Okay. No butterfly then?

ORLA. No.

LIAM. Fair enough.

LIAM *puts the butterfly back in its jar but then pauses.*

But Orla, the thing is . . .

ORLA. What?

LIAM. I think it'd be better if I did it.

ORLA. It'll work fine without it.

LIAM. But Man in White has to do something extreme.

ORLA. I don't want you to do it.

LIAM. You're not getting what I'm saying.

ORLA. Liam, I don't care.

LIAM. It says something about life then. When a relationship's
dead, it's dead.

ORLA. It's fine the other way.

LIAM. But it's not, Orla.

ORLA. You said killing something for a film was wrong.

LIAM. I thought you were just being arty-farty then. But I get
it now.

ORLA. Use the plastic butterfly. It makes no difference.

LIAM. But that won't capture anything of the . . . the pain, the
fuckin' . . . heartache of real life.

ORLA. Liam, it's my film and I'm saying no.

LIAM. Why?

ORLA. Because.

LIAM. You want it to be good, don't you?

ORLA (*hesitates*). Yes.

LIAM. 100 per cent committed, you said.

ORLA. I know what I said.

LIAM. Did you mean it?

ORLA. Of course I did.

LIAM. So why don't you want to do it?

ORLA. It's complicated.

LIAM. Why is it complicated?

ORLA. Why? Why? Why? It's always 'Why?' with you! Like you're a little child or something. This is my decision, Liam. There's a chain of command and I'm the director and that's how it works!

LIAM. Why?

ORLA. Christ, Liam!

LIAM. I just want an answer, Orla. What's your problem?

ORLA. You're my problem.

LIAM. That's hardly 100 per cent, Orla.

ORLA. I said no.

LIAM. 70 per cent and falling . . .

ORLA. Things are different now.

LIAM. 50, tops.

ORLA. Liam, I said no!

LIAM. But why?

ORLA. Because!

LIAM. Because what?!

ORLA (*upset*). I don't want it to die, okay!?

> ORLA *sits on the sofa. A beat.* LIAM *turns on the lights.*

LIAM (*shrugs*). Okay, Orla. Jesus . . .

> ORLA *says nothing.* LIAM *sighs and puts down the jar. He sits beside her and sees how upset she is.*

Sorry . . . It's just . . . (*Shakes his head.*) It doesn't matter . . .

ORLA. What?

LIAM. I don't know, it's weird but for the first time I felt like I was getting your film. Like it was all suddenly clicking into place and you catch a glimpse of the big picture, y'know? . . . Like . . . like when you realise Bruce Willis is dead at the end of *The Sixth Sense*?

> LIAM *looks to* ORLA *for a response.* ORLA, *still upset, says nothing.*

I like your haircut, by the way.

ORLA (*touching her hair*). Sorry?

LIAM. Your new haircut. It's nice.

ORLA (*touched*). I didn't think you noticed.

LIAM. It suits you.

> *A beat.*

ORLA. Say that bit again: 'Lost in the night, no more.'

LIAM. Why?

ORLA. Just do it.

LIAM. Lost in the night, no more.

ORLA. Ten years of writing poetry and watching films have led me to this moment right now. But here I am with you and . . . I'm not thinking about art.

LIAM. You've lost me.

ORLA. You've found me.

> ORLA *touches* LIAM*'s hand.*

LIAM. Eh, Orla.

ORLA. You're the only one in the class who understands me, Liam.

LIAM. But I don't understand you.

ORLA. When you say it.

LIAM. Look, Orla –

ORLA. Lost in the night, no more . . .

LIAM. Maybe we should –

ORLA. Your lips curl up . . .

LIAM. Orla, I don't –

ORLA. . . . In the cutest way.

> ORLA *stops. She sees how terrified* LIAM *is.* ORLA, *mortified, gets up and walks away from him.*

LIAM. It's . . . it's not you, Orla.

ORLA (*laughs nervously*). I'm sorry, Liam, I don't know what I'm doing.

> LIAM *gets up and goes to her.*

LIAM. No really, I mean it.

ORLA. Everything was so different when I was younger. Even though it was just the two of us, I used to love coming home and finding what bizarre new recipe Dad had tried. Stuffed herrings with apples, dandelion and bacon salad . . .

LIAM. Orla . . . what are you talking about?

ORLA (*laughs nervously*). God, all the time I've spent on this film and now it seems so unimportant, so meaningless in the face of Dad having . . . God, I can barely even say it.

LIAM. Say what?

ORLA. Cancer.

LIAM. Eh, Orla . . .

ORLA (*shrugs, close to tears*). Baked halibut with a pumpkin crust. That was my favourite.

LIAM. Orla, your dad doesn't have cancer.

ORLA. Sorry?

LIAM. He made it up.

ORLA (*bewildered*). But . . . What? How do you know?

LIAM. This afternoon, he told me he wanted to stay. And he said maybe he could pretend to be dying so that you'd let him.

ORLA (*shouts*). Dad!

LIAM. I told him not to.

GERARD *enters, carrying the clapperboard.*

GERARD. Oops! I spotted this in my room. I must have accidentally used it as a tray when I was taking tea and biscuits up earlier. I only just noticed it now. What a nincompoop I am!

LIAM *and* ORLA *stare at* GERARD *blankly. A beat. He puts the clapperboard down.*

(*Cheerful.*) So, I'll leave you to it!

ORLA. Dad, don't go.

GERARD. Sorry?

ORLA. How will I know when to wear a jacket?

GERARD. Excuse me?

ORLA. How will I avoid catching my death of cold? I don't know when it's cold out or not.

GERARD. I'm not following you.

ORLA. Of course most people simply look out the window and guess what to wear, and they usually don't die of pneumonia but I'm not like that.

GERARD (*to* LIAM). What is she talking about?

LIAM. Orla.

ORLA (*to* GERARD). If you're not here, I won't know when to put it on. Should I wear it now? Should I put my jacket on now? I should, shouldn't I?

ORLA *puts her jacket on and stands defiantly before a bewildered* GERARD. *A beat.*

GERARD (*blankly*). I have no response to that.

ORLA. You don't? Maybe I should wear two, would that be better? Otherwise I might get a chill and fall down dead on the spot. Thanks, that's the kind of propitious advice I need.

ORLA *puts* LIAM*'s jacket on over her own.* GERARD *and* LIAM *stare at her.*

It's not like you'd have to tell a grown adult to wear her jacket when she leaves the house. You'd only say that to a child, wouldn't you? Am I right? . . . (*Louder.*) Am I right?

GERARD (*to* ORLA). Orla, have you completely lost your marbles?

LIAM (*to* GERARD). This is my fault.

ORLA. No, it's not, Liam. (*Pointing at* GERARD.) It's his.

GERARD. What is my fault? Will you please tell me what is going on here?

ORLA. Dad, you don't have cancer.

GERARD. What? . . . What do you mean, Orla?

ORLA. Dad, give it a rest, please?

GERARD. Okay, Orla, okay. You're right. (*Pause.*) Maybe I don't have cancer . . . but maybe I do. I won't know until the doctor rings with the results.

ORLA. Which doctor?

GERARD. He wasn't a witch doctor! He was a fully licenced cancer specialist.

ORLA. Dr O'Connell, was it?

GERARD. No, no. This was a special clinic I went to. Out near Greystones. You wouldn't know it.

ORLA. What's it called?

LIAM. Orla, listen. Will you sit down and let me explain what's going on.

ORLA *ignores him.*

GERARD. Tell me, Orla, why would I make up something like this?

GERARD *waits for a response.* ORLA *walks away, saying nothing.* GERARD *goes over to her and stands in front of her.*

(*Serious.*) No, Orla, look at me. I want to know why you would think that. What kind of a man do you think I am?

ORLA (*unsure*). Didn't you tell Liam that you were going to lie to me?

GERARD (*laughs*). You believe the word of this boy over your own father?! He's been lying to you all weekend!

ORLA. What?

GERARD. He's not your friend, Orla. He doesn't care about you! He's only here because it'll help him get his ex-girlfriend back.

ORLA *looks at* LIAM. *He looks away.*

ORLA (*to* LIAM). You were using me?

LIAM. No, Orla, let me explain. I . . . I didn't want to hurt your feelings.

GERARD (*to* ORLA). You see? I knew from the start you couldn't trust him!

ORLA (*to* GERARD). Why did you lie to me, Dad?

GERARD. Orla, you have it all wrong. Yes, I did say to Liam I was going to tell you I was dying. But I only said that because it's the truth. Liam assumed it was a lie but it's not. It's the truth, Orla. The doctor will ring and then you'll see . . . (*He notices the butterfly jar and picks it up.*) Is this for your film? You'll need to get a bigger jar if you want it to live.

ORLA. What did you say the clinic was called?

GERARD. My God, Orla! Why all the questions? I tell you I'm dying and you hold a table quiz!

ORLA. I'm in shock . . . What's the clinic called, Dad?

GERARD. I don't remember. Did you know that butterflies taste through their feet? Can't be very hygienic, can it?

ORLA. When did you go to this clinic?

GERARD. The Hartzell Clinic! That's what it's called. Out near Greystones. So now, do you believe me, Orla?

*A beat.*

ORLA (*quietly*). Yes, Dad. I do.

*A beat.*

(*To* LIAM.) Well, that's a relief.

GERARD. What?

ORLA (*to* LIAM). After getting my hopes up that he might be dying, it would've been awful if it wasn't true.

GERARD. Orla, what are you saying?

ORLA (*to* LIAM). I was so disappointed when you said he was lying. But now I know it's true. You don't know how happy that makes me. Now all we have to do is wait. Fingers crossed!

GERARD *is stunned.* ORLA *glances at him.*

LIAM. Jesus, Orla!

ORLA. What?

*Behind them,* GERARD, *still holding the butterfly jar, goes into the kitchen and locks the door.*

LIAM. How can you be so heartless? You don't really want him to die, do you?

ORLA *notices* GERARD *has gone into the kitchen. She turns to* LIAM.

ORLA. Of course not. He doesn't have cancer, Liam.

LIAM. But you just said . . .

ORLA. The Hartzell Clinic? Mr Hartzell is the name of the
English teacher in *Catcher in the Rye*, which Dad's teaching
for the Leaving this year. He's making it all up.

ORLA *walks over to the kitchen door.*

Dad?

GERARD, *agitated, paces in the kitchen.*

Dad, open the door.

LIAM. But why did you say those things to him?

ORLA. He started it.

LIAM. Jesus Christ! Will you listen to me, Orla? You don't
know the whole story.

ORLA. And you do, right? The big game player holding all the
cards! Well, something tells me your plan to get Nicole isn't
going to work.

LIAM. What? . . . Why not?

ORLA. It's not my fault, Liam. You shouldn't have lied to me.

LIAM. What did you say to her?

ORLA. Only that you think she's a frigid bitch who needs lots
of make-up.

LIAM (*furious*). What!?

ORLA. I was only repeating what you said.

LIAM. Jesus Christ, Orla!

ORLA. I was only trying to convince her because she wouldn't
believe you were working on my film. I didn't know you
wanted to get back together in copasetic bliss!

LIAM. You did this on purpose!

ORLA. No, you told me you wanted revenge.

LIAM. You were only supposed to tell her I was helping you!

ORLA. But Liam, sometimes it's good to talk. Better not to keep it all inside? Isn't that what you said to me, Liam? Isn't it?

*LIAM grabs his jacket and heads for the exit. He turns to ORLA.*

LIAM. Fuck you, Orla. Fuck you and your poxy movie!

ORLA (*shouts*). It's not a movie, it's a film!

*Suddenly the phone in the kitchen rings. Everyone freezes. A beat. GERARD answers the phone.*

*Lights go down.*

## ACT THREE

*Sunday morning. The living room is the same as it was last night.* GERARD *sits in the kitchen, his head in his hands, the butterfly jar beside him.* ORLA *enters, carrying a plastic bag containing a Scart lead.*

ORLA (*jolly*). Brrr! Chilly out, this morning.

GERARD (*looks up*). Orla?

> ORLA *takes off her jacket and a script out of her back pocket. She tosses it onto the table and goes to the kitchen door.*

ORLA. I have a little surprise for you, Dad. I went and bought a Scart lead. So now I can hook up the DVD and we can watch films on it. Isn't that good news?

> *No answer.*

> Could you come out and give me a hand with it?

> *A beat.*

GERARD. We don't have any DVDs to play on it.

ORLA. I'll buy some later.

GERARD (*loud*). Excuse me?

ORLA (*loud*). I said I'd buy some later.

GERARD. If you're going out, then wrap up well.

> ORLA, *thinking, paces around the room. She goes to the kitchen door again.*

ORLA. How about some breakfast? Are you hungry, Dad?

GERARD. Not really.

ORLA. I was hoping you'd make me some French toast.

GERARD. Excuse me?

ORLA (*loud*). French toast.

GERARD *says nothing.*

You know I love the way you make it. With cinnamon and honey. How about it?

GERARD. Did you know that French toast didn't actually originate in France? It was invented by an American called Joseph French in the eighteenth century.

ORLA, *annoyed, throws the Scart lead onto the sofa.*

Did you say something?

ORLA (*innocently*). No . . . Dad? . . . It's been ages since we've been up to Kilmainham. Why don't we go today? Wouldn't that be nice? Spending an afternoon strolling around the exhibits? You giving out about the art, me giving out about parents letting their children run around? Then we could go for overpriced cream teas in the Westbury and both give out about that. Wouldn't that be fun?

GERARD. It's been so long since we've had a day like that.

ORLA. Why don't we do it today?

GERARD. When?

ORLA. Now.

*A beat.*

GERARD. I thought it was cold out.

ORLA. Not *that* cold.

GERARD. Chilly out, you said.

ORLA. I was exaggerating.

GERARD. I don't want to catch a cold . . . Surely that wouldn't be wise when we don't know what the prognosis is.

ORLA (*annoyed*). We can wear our winter coats.

*A beat.* GERARD *stands up and moves to the door.*

GERARD (*gently*). You know, Orla, whenever I suggest you put on a jacket, I'm not doing it to patronise you. I'm not trying to demean you. I'm only saying it because I care about you.

ORLA (*sighs*). Dad, will you open the door and give me the butterfly? . . . Please? I need it.

GERARD. Is that what this rigmarole is all about? French toast and Scart leads! If you wanted the butterfly, why didn't you simply ask me for it?

ORLA. I asked you for it hours ago.

GERARD. But you can't shoot it without Liam anyway, so what difference does it make?

ORLA. Change of plan. I'll shoot a close-up of me killing the butterfly and intercut it with the footage of Liam.

GERARD. So you still want to finish your film? . . . Even after last night?

ORLA. Dad, last night . . . when I said I was relieved you might die, you didn't think I was being serious, did you?

ORLA *waits for a response.* GERARD *says nothing.*

Because I wasn't. You know how I can get. I was annoyed because the film wasn't going right . . . I don't want you to die, Dad.

GERARD. Honestly?

ORLA (*paces as she talks*). Yes. I was . . . blowing off steam . . . I was being silly.

GERARD. Then I hope you didn't get a fright when the phone rang last night.

ORLA. Oh no, I guessed it was Nicole. Who else would ring at that hour, only a drunken twit desperate for a ride?

GERARD. And I couldn't make any sense of Liam's plan. It seemed like gibberish to me but he got the girl in the end . . .

ORLA *goes over to the kitchen door.*

ORLA (*glumly*). They're probably having breakfast at the moment, eating croissants and reading the Sunday papers . . .

or at least the *Beano*. God, he couldn't run out of here fast enough after she rang. Away from the freak show . . . They're probably laughing at us right now.

GERARD (*gently*). Orla, they're beneath our contempt . . .

ORLA. Sorry?

GERARD (*loud*). I said they're beneath our contempt!

*A beat.*

ORLA. So, can I have it?

GERARD. It means a lot to you, does it? This film?

ORLA. It's the most important thing in the world to me. Dad, all I want is to get this last shot.

GERARD (*unsure*). And you honestly didn't mean what you said last night?

ORLA. No, Dad. I didn't.

GERARD. Can I read your script?

*ORLA freezes.*

ORLA. What?

GERARD. Your script. Can I read it?

ORLA. No.

GERARD. Why not?

ORLA. You know I don't like showing my work until it's finished.

GERARD. Orla, I know the film's about me.

ORLA (*panicked*). No, it isn't!

*ORLA paces nervously.*

GERARD. It's not?

ORLA (*laughs nervously*). No, why do you say that?

GERARD. Why don't you want me to read it then?

ORLA (*nervous*). But you always wait till my film's finished before watching it. Why change that pattern of behaviour now? Why introduce that element of random chaos into our lives when there's enough uncertainty in modern living as it is?

GERARD. Orla, you're rambling.

ORLA. I'm trying to explain.

GERARD. Well, stop explaining and simply tell me.

*ORLA takes the script off the table and hides it under the dollhouse roof.*

ORLA. I can't find it. Liam must've taken it.

GERARD. Orla, why won't you give me your script?

*ORLA goes over to the kitchen.*

ORLA. Dad, I'm telling you the truth, Liam took the only copy . . . Open the door and see for yourself if you don't believe me.

GERARD. But why would he do that?

ORLA. Who knows? Maybe he was angry? Maybe he was –

*The doorbell rings. ORLA freezes. It rings again, insistently.*

GERARD. Are you going to get that?

*ORLA anxiously exits.*

LIAM (*offstage*). Well, here I am again!

*A slightly drunk LIAM enters. He paces around the room, angry and hyper. ORLA follows.*

ORLA. Liam. Wait a minute, my dad is going to ask you –

LIAM (*ignoring her*). A glutton for punishment, that's me!

*GERARD gets up and goes to the kitchen door.*

GERARD. Liam?

ORLA (*to LIAM*). Stop, I have to tell you something.

LIAM. Orla, I don't want to hear it.

ORLA. God, I can smell the drink off you. It's not even twelve.

GERARD (*loud*). Liam?

LIAM *looks around him, not sure where the voice is coming from.*

(*Loud.*) Did you take Orla's script last night?

ORLA (*to* LIAM). Say yes. I'll explain later.

LIAM (*to* ORLA). Why should I do anything you ask me?

GERARD (*loud*). Well? Did you take it? Hello?

ORLA. Please, Liam.

LIAM. You know I said I liked your haircut?

ORLA. Yes?

LIAM. Well, I lied. Training day at barber college, was it?

ORLA. Take that back.

LIAM. It's a question, I can't take it back.

GERARD. Excuse me?

ORLA (*loudly to* GERARD). Dad, he's drunk. He doesn't even know where he is!

LIAM. I'm not drunk. I've been drinking. That's not the same as drunk.

ORLA. You drink too much.

LIAM. You don't drink enough.

GERARD (*loud*). Liam, did you take Orla's script last night?

LIAM (*loud*). Yeah, I really wanted a souvenir of this tremendous weekend!

ORLA (*loud*). Don't mind him, Dad. It's an in-joke we have.

LIAM. No, it's not. I didn't touch your precious script.

GERARD, *dismayed, sits at the table again.*

ORLA. Dad? . . . Dad?

GERARD *doesn't answer. He looks at the butterfly in the jar.* LIAM *paces, agitated.*

(*To* LIAM.) Thanks a bunch, Liam!

LIAM. All weekend I help you with your movie and what thanks do I get? You sabotage me and Nicole.

ORLA. You were the one who lied to me!

LIAM (*ignores her*). But that wasn't enough. Couldn't let me have my happy ending, could you?

ORLA *walks over to the exit and shows* LIAM *the way out.*

ORLA. What a poignant synopsis, Liam, but if you don't mind, I have a film to finish.

LIAM. This isn't the way it's supposed to be. Nicole should be waking me up right now by stroking my foot with her toes . . . She liked doing that.

ORLA. Liam, what do you want?

LIAM. It's your fault.

ORLA. What is my fault?

LIAM. Acting in your movie, trying my best to say that ridiculous speech, making a fool of myself. And after all that, when it finally clicks why I should kill the butterfly, you go and change your mind. No wonder I was so screwed up.

ORLA. What happened last night?

LIAM *looks at* ORLA *and sighs. He sits on the sofa.*

LIAM. I went to Doyles where Nicole was having her party. She was in this tiny pink top and covered in sweat from dancing but God, she was a total vision. Like Katie Holmes in *The Gift* or Carla Gu-whatsherface –

ORLA. I get the picture.

LIAM. So we had a pint and I was explaining how I didn't really mean any of the stuff you told her I said when her favourite song came on. The Violent Femmes' 'Blister in the Sun'?

ORLA *shrugs; she doesn't know it.*

So she dragged me up on the dance floor and everyone was jumping so wildly, I could feel the wooden floor creaking and bouncing from the weight. And just when I thought we might literally bring the house down, she put her arms around me and we kissed. And I swear it was like fucking 75-frames-a-second slow-motion. There we were, holding each other in the middle of the dance floor, heaving bodies flying around us, a strobe flashing above and the earth moving beneath our feet.

ORLA (*glum*). Sounds like fun.

LIAM. Then we went back to her place. It was so perfect . . . or at least it would have been if it wasn't for you.

ORLA. What did I do?

LIAM. You got me so tangled up in your movie that I couldn't get it out of my head.

ORLA. I don't understand.

LIAM. Why? Because I don't have the big, intelligent words you use? Is that it? All the words you've been throwing at me this weekend, trying to make me feel like an idiot?

ORLA. I wasn't trying.

LIAM *throws her a look. He gets up and faces* ORLA.

LIAM. Come on. What are we waiting for? Let's do it.

ORLA. Do what?

LIAM. Finish your movie.

ORLA (*incredulous*). You want to finish my film?

LIAM. Yes.

ORLA. Why?

LIAM. Because then the problem will be solved and I can go back to Nicole.

ORLA. What problem?

LIAM *walks away from* ORLA.

LIAM. It doesn't matter. Let's just do this so I can get out of here.

ORLA. What happened with Nicole? What was my fault?

LIAM. You don't need to know.

ORLA. I do.

LIAM (*annoyed*). Can we just finish the movie, please?

ORLA. No. Not until you tell me the whole story. You think I trust you for one second after last night? Now what was my fault?

LIAM. Fine, Orla, you want to know? (*He puts his face into hers.*) It was your fault I couldn't fucking get it up last night. Happy now?

LIAM *walks away from her.*

ORLA (*incredulous*). How on earth is that my fault?

LIAM. Because I couldn't get your movie out of my head, I couldn't relax and I couldn't . . . perform in the bedroom.

ORLA. I'm sorry, what?

LIAM. D'you know how long I'd been dreaming of that moment? That moment before sex where nothing else matters and all your worries melt away and time crawls to a complete stop? And last night, I was back on her bed with her lips on mine and my fingers on her back and Nicole popping the buttons on my jeans. And even though she'd been dancing all night, her skin still smelled like cherries. And if you were thinking more fully you'd wish that that moment would last forever but you're not even thinking that deeply, you don't care coz the only thing that matters is her body and the parts of it that are touching yours. Except . . . that's what I should have been thinking. Do you know what was actually going through my head?

ORLA. What?

LIAM. If Man in White doesn't kill the butterfly then Broken Doll will never realise how empty her life is and nothing will ever change for her!

ORLA *stares at* LIAM, *speechless. A beat. He continues.*

No matter what I tried, I couldn't stop thinking about your movie. And when I tried to explain this to Nicole, she got it all wrong and thought I was saying I couldn't get you out of my head. And I told her I'd rather chew glass than be in bed with you but I couldn't make her understand so she kicked me out.

ORLA. And do you have this problem often?

LIAM (*firm*). Don't start.

ORLA (*innocently*). I'm only asking.

LIAM. Last night was so perfect. It wasn't supposed to turn out like this.

ORLA. Life's a fiasco, Liam. Get used to it.

LIAM. No, I can still make this right. This isn't me! This isn't how it goes.

ORLA. Liam, believe me, I know what I'm talking about. Life is not perfect.

LIAM. You're just giving up. But that's not who I am . . . So if we just put the movie to bed, it'll be complete in my head and I can forget about it. I'll have my closure and the problem will go away.

ORLA. Liam, I don't know why you think my film has anything to do with your impotence.

LIAM. I'm not impotent! This never happened to me before.

ORLA. But there could be any number of reasons for it. Why fixate on my film?

LIAM. Shut up, that's why.

ORLA *throws her arms in the air.*

ORLA. Fine, Liam. If you want to help me, that's great. Let's do it.

LIAM. You get the camera, I'll set up the lights.

ORLA. But we can't finish it.

LIAM. Why not?

ORLA. Dad has the butterfly in there and he's locked the door. We can't do the last scene without it.

LIAM. I thought you weren't going to kill it. What changed your mind?

ORLA. Finding out my dad is a selfish bastard! I want the butterfly to die screaming in intense pain.

LIAM. I don't think butterflies scream.

ORLA (*shrugs*). I'll dub it on later.

LIAM (*looks at the kitchen*). Can you get in through the window?

ORLA. It's locked.

LIAM. Do you have a spare key for the door?

ORLA (*surprised*). I never even thought of that.

ORLA *exits.*

LIAM (*to* GERARD). Hello? (*No answer.*) Mr Cullen?

GERARD. Are you talking to me?

LIAM. What are you doing in there?

GERARD. Excuse me?

LIAM (*loud*). What are you doing in there?

GERARD (*shakes his head, weary*). Don't ask me. Where's Orla?

LIAM. She's gone upstairs. Can I get the butterfly off you, please?

GERARD. Why? So you can finish her film, then take a front-row seat to laugh it off the screen?

LIAM. Look, if Orla wants to be an artist, she has to take a bit of stick.

GERARD. It'll destroy her.

LIAM. You have to let her make her own mistakes. She's not – hang on! I thought you wanted the film finished.

GERARD. What am I supposed to believe? Orla makes a tribute film to me but then wishes I was dead? She tells me she didn't mean it but then lies and says you took her script! How am I to make sense of it all? Why can't she simply be honest with me?

LIAM. Oh, come on! You lied about having cancer.

GERARD (*outraged*). I did not!

LIAM. Orla said you named the clinic after someone in *Catcher in the Rye* or something?

*A beat.*

GERARD (*quietly*). Orla told you that?

LIAM. Yeah, look, she knows it's all a big lie. That's why she's been acting so crazy . . . But if you just open the door and let us finish the film, I'm telling you, everything'll be grand.

GERARD *leaps up and goes to the door.*

GERARD (*angry*). Everything will be grand, will it?! What do you know about life? What do you know about being a father? A girl ditches you and you think it's the end of the world. You've no idea what life is actually like. I've already lost my wife, I can't stand by and lose my daughter too!

*A beat.*

LIAM (*confused*). What?

GERARD *walks away from the door. He paces in the kitchen.*

GERARD. If I don't take steps now, she'll be gone and I'll be left here by myself. Year in, year out, watching *Countdown* on my own, reading the obits and slowly, inevitably crumbling away into nothing.

*A beat.*

LIAM. That's the real reason you're doing this? But . . . that's nuts.

GERARD. Your plan was crazy and it worked.

LIAM. What plan?

GERARD. Getting Orla to ring Nicole.

LIAM. My plan wasn't crazy . . . So you stop Orla from graduating this year, what are you going to do next year?

GERARD (*shrugs*). I'll cross that bridge when I get to it.

LIAM. But . . . you're blackmailing Orla into staying with you. That's just wrong.

GERARD *sits down again.*

GERARD. I'm not blackmailing her, I'm helping her.

LIAM. No, you're not.

GERARD. I'm doing it for her own good.

LIAM. You're doing it for yourself, you nut-job!

GERARD (*chuckles dismissively*). No, no. You don't understand.

LIAM (*incredulous*). But you just said ten seconds ago you didn't want to be alone.

GERARD. You don't appreciate the relationship Orla and I have. Things are strained this weekend but they'll be back to normal soon enough. As long as I shield her from the humiliation. That's the important thing.

LIAM. But that's just an excuse because you don't want her to leave . . . Do you realise that after this weekend, Orla will never speak to you again? I know normally that'd be a good thing but is it really what you want?

GERARD. You wouldn't understand . . . That's not an insult by the way, I mean it literally.

LIAM. How can I get it through to you?

GERARD (*laughs*). There's nothing to get.

LIAM *paces, thinking.*

LIAM. You want to spare Orla from humiliation? That's why you're doing this?

GERARD. Yes.

LIAM. So why not come out and help her with the film? Make sure there's nothing in it to laugh at?

GERARD. How can I do that when she won't even let me read her script?

LIAM *looks around for the script. He looks under the dollhouse roof, finds it and slides it under the kitchen door.*

LIAM. There. Now you've no excuse.

ORLA *enters, looking at her fingernail. In the kitchen,* GERARD *stares at the script a moment, then picks it up, sits at the table and reads it.*

ORLA (*to* LIAM). Any luck?

LIAM (*weary*). I don't know. Did you find a spare key?

ORLA (*holds up her nail*). All I got was a bloody broken nail from rooting around the top of the wardrobe. (*Sighs, weary.*) God, I'm worn out by him!

ORLA *goes over to the kitchen.*

Dad?

*No answer.*

Dad, will you please open up? . . . Are you not even going to talk to me now?

GERARD, *absorbed in reading the script, doesn't answer.* ORLA *sighs, defeated. She turns back to* LIAM.

Why did you say it then?

LIAM. What?

ORLA. Why did you say you liked my haircut if you didn't mean it?

LIAM. Because at the time I thought you needed to hear something nice.

ORLA (*listens at the door again*). What do you think he's doing in there?

LIAM. Reading.

ORLA. Reading what?

LIAM. Your script.

ORLA (*horrified*). You gave him my script?

LIAM. Yes.

ORLA. Why did you do that?!

LIAM. So he'd open the door.

ORLA. Dad?

    GERARD, *absorbed in reading, doesn't answer.*

    I can't believe you'd do that, Liam!

LIAM (*baffled*). What do you mean?

ORLA. That you'd be this malicious!

LIAM (*baffled*). I was trying to get the butterfly. Isn't that what you wanted?

ORLA. Don't plead ignorance! You knew exactly what you were doing! Getting me to look for a spare key so that you'd have your chance?

LIAM (*incredulous*). I don't believe this.

ORLA. All part of your master plan.

LIAM. What master plan?! Didn't you want the butterfly?!

ORLA. After I bare my soul and confide in you, what do you do? Betray me and fling it back in my face!

LIAM. Jesus Christ! Are we all on different fucking planets?! What the hell are you talking about?

    ORLA, *fuming, walks over to the fish tank, pulls the cow's heart out of it and holds it up to* LIAM. *She walks to the bin and throws it in. She gives* LIAM *a defiant look. He stares back at her in disbelief.*

    What the hell is that supposed to mean?!

ORLA (*calm*). You can forget about the film now, Liam.

LIAM. Orla, you said.

ORLA. I changed my mind.

LIAM. Jesus, for once in your life will you do something for someone else?

ORLA. Liam, I *could* care less . . . but not much.

LIAM. Orla, I need this. It's important.

ORLA. I said no.

LIAM. You don't get it, do you? You don't get how much Nicole means to me.

ORLA. Oh spare me!

LIAM. You can't comprehend how someone else can feel this much about another human being. What would you know about people with your Maya Derren videos and your fuckin' amniotic brine?

ORLA. And don't worry about your little problem Liam, I'll give Mr Viagra your number next time I see him!

LIAM. Can't even admit you cried at *E.T.*? Can't deal with any kind of human feelings at all, can you?

ORLA. Get it through your thick fucking skull, Liam, I did not cry at *E.T.*

LIAM. I was sitting right behind you, Orla! Why can't you admit it? What is wrong with you?

*A beat.*

ORLA. Okay, Liam. Yes, I was crying. I was crying and you saw me . . . But it had nothing to do with that moronic film. I wasn't even watching it, I was crying because all day not one person said a single word about my stupid new haircut . . . Oh, I know what you're all like, and on the way in last Tuesday I was bracing myself for the reaction. For the quips and the jibes but then I get there and there's not a word. Not a snigger. Not even a look . . . The whole day went by and not one person in the class even noticed my hair. Because they didn't see me . . . Because I'm invisible,

I don't even exist . . . I am nothing . . . That's why I was crying, Liam. It had nothing to do with *E.* bloody *T.*

*A beat.*

LIAM. Orla, we have to finish the movie. I can't go on without Nicole.

ORLA. God, Liam, will you listen to yourself?

LIAM. Are you going to do it?

ORLA. There's more chance of you winning an Oscar this year.

*LIAM grabs the dollhouse by the roof and yanks it to the ground. The contents go sprawling.*

LIAM. I'm not kidding, Orla! She's the only thing I care about.

ORLA. You don't give a shit about Nicole. Every time you talk about her, it's never how funny *she* is or how great *she* is, it's always about how she laughs at *your* jokes or how she encourages *you.* '*I* can't keep going without her. *I* don't care about anything else. *I* deserve her.' You don't see her as a person. You don't care about her. You only care about how she makes you feel.

LIAM (*unsure*). That's . . . that's not true.

ORLA. Tell me, Liam, what's Nicole's graduate film about? Do you even know? And how was her shoot? Did you bother to ask her? Well, did you?

*LIAM sits on the sofa, the fight gone out of him. ORLA goes over to the kitchen.*

(*Scared but hopeful.*) Dad?

*No answer. In the kitchen, GERARD finishes reading the script and puts it down.*

(*Louder.*) Dad?

GERARD. Yes, Orla?

ORLA. Did you . . . did you read it?

GERARD. Yes, Orla, I did.

*A beat.*

ORLA (*hopeful*). And . . . ?

GERARD. I'm not sure what to say.

ORLA. Dad, I can explain.

GERARD. I have to say, Orla, I'm disappointed.

ORLA. You were never supposed to see it.

GERARD. That's no excuse, Orla.

ORLA. It's only made up. You shouldn't take it seriously.

GERARD. No matter, Orla, there has to be some sense to it.

ORLA. Dad, I'm sorry. I didn't . . . What? . . . What do you mean?

GERARD. Just because it's fiction doesn't mean you can throw out the rule book on logic.

ORLA. I'm not following. You read my script?

GERARD. Yes.

ORLA. And you understood it?

GERARD (*shrugs*). The gist of it . . .

ORLA. What didn't you understand?

GERARD. I don't know what I was expecting, really. I hoped it would give me some kind of an insight into how you see me. How you see our life together. I wasn't expecting what reads, for all the world, like the . . . random thoughts of a paranoid monkey. I'm not trying to be funny, that's my honest impression of it.

ORLA (*crestfallen*). You didn't understand it?

GERARD. What's it supposed to be about? Is it a lament for lost youth? A diatribe against patriarchy? A polemic against cruelty to insects? What has all of that got to do with me?

ORLA (*hurt*). How can you not understand it, Dad? I put so much into it. I thought . . . I thought it would . . .

GERARD. It would what?

ORLA. Nothing.

GERARD. You're disappointed?

ORLA. Out of everyone in the whole world . . . If anyone was going to understand it, I thought it would be you.

GERARD. If it's any consolation, I understand why you didn't want me to see it. But Orla, you can't blame your audience if they don't understand your film, am I right?

ORLA (*defeated*). Yes, Dad . . . You're right.

ORLA *sits on the floor, beaten.*

GERARD. Now feel free to disagree, Orla, but I think you should shelve this version altogether and perhaps aim to have a film ready for next year instead. I can help with it, give you guidance throughout the year . . . You'll see I'm right in the future . . .

LIAM (*loudly*). She has no future!

GERARD *and* ORLA *freeze in surprised bafflement.* ORLA *looks at* LIAM. GERARD *listens at the door.* LIAM *lifts his head and continues, passionately.*

No chance to soar!

LIAM *stands up and continues.*

Her wings will become dust behind a locked door,
Her heart is no more, worn out by strife,
Her taciturn scream, lost in the night,
No more dreams, no nothing, no life . . .

*The words strike a chord with* GERARD. *A beat. He picks up the butterfly jar, and comes out of the kitchen.* ORLA *stares at him, not knowing what to say.*

GERARD (*chuckles*). Once, when you were only small, I spent a whole afternoon taking apart the TV remote control after it suddenly stopped working. I had batteries and wires spread all over the kitchen table and then your mother walked in. And she asked me what I was doing with the remote for the CD player . . . You never see the woods for the trees, she used to say to me.

*A beat.*

ORLA. I miss her.

GERARD. I do too, Orla . . .

GERARD. If she was here right now she would've understood your film in an instant. Would have seen how rich and meaningful it is . . . And she would've called me a self-indulgent fool . . . Only she's not here any more . . . But you are, Orla. And the thought of losing you makes me do stupid things. Stupid selfish things that even a child wouldn't do . . . You're all I have, Orla.

GERARD *looks to* ORLA *for a response. She doesn't know what to say.*

You know I lied about having cancer too, don't you?

ORLA (*embarrassed*). Yes, Dad.

GERARD. I don't know why I did that, Orla. It popped out of my mouth before I could stop myself and then I just kept digging myself deeper and deeper . . . I'm sorry for doing that, Orla.

ORLA. I know, Dad.

GERARD. And I'm sorry for locking myself in the bathroom at Christmas.

ORLA. I know, Dad.

GERARD. And I'm sorry for scaring off your original actor.

ORLA. I kn– . . . What?

GERARD (*embarrassed*). I may have ever so slightly threatened him when he was over rehearsing last weekend. But he was a lecherous little creep, Orla, you can't deny that.

ORLA *shakes her head in disbelief.*

But that . . . that kind of behaviour is behind me now. I promise.

ORLA. I'm not a child any more.

GERARD. Things will change around here, Orla. From now on. I mean it.

ORLA. Dad, I . . . I can't spend the rest of my life watching films with you here but that doesn't mean I don't want you in my life . . . You're all I have too . . . My life will change and so will yours but it'll be okay. It'll be different, that's all.

GERARD (*holds up butterfly jar*). Like a caterpillar changing into a butterfly?

ORLA *smiles.* GERARD *hands her the jar.*

I think maybe I'll go and have lunch at Carmel's. Perhaps I should do it every weekend? Give the old bat someone to moan at.

GERARD *starts to leave.*

ORLA. Dad?

GERARD. Yes, Orla?

ORLA. It is a bit chilly out.

ORLA *holds up* GERARD's *jacket.* GERARD *goes over to her and puts it on.*

GERARD. Don't want to catch my death of cold now, do I?

GERARD *exits.*

LIAM (*excited*). God, all this time it was staring me in the face and I didn't see it. How many times did I read it and all I saw was pretentious wank? But I wasn't looking hard enough. What the butterfly represents . . . It's you . . . (*A beat.*) And did you see the effect it had on him? It was your words that made him come out of the kitchen.

ORLA. No, it wasn't, Liam . . . It was yours.

LIAM. But to be able to reach someone like that . . . really speak to them, y'know? It's amazing . . . I had no idea you could do that with words. With stuff you write yourself.

ORLA (*surprised and delighted*). Hello? Isn't that what I've been saying to you all week? I told you, Liam. Art is important.

ORLA *puts the dollhouse the right way up.*

LIAM. Sorry about that, by the way. Is it worth a lot?

ORLA (*waves her hand dismissively*). I lied, it's a piece of junk.

LIAM *holds up the butterfly jar.*

LIAM. So what are we waiting for? Let's do this.

ORLA (*nods*). You get changed and set up the lights. I'll get the camera.

LIAM *puts on the white shirt and picks up the clapperboard.* ORLA *sets up the camera but then pauses and looks at the butterfly jar.*

You know what, Liam? Let's use the plastic butterfly instead.

LIAM. Yeah?

ORLA. Some quick editing and you'll never notice. (*Holds up the jar*). I think she's been through enough this weekend.

LIAM (*shrugs*). You're the director.

ORLA *and* LIAM *go into the kitchen.* ORLA *opens the kitchen window, then lifts up the jar.*

ORLA. That's a wrap for you, little one.

*She opens the jar and lets the butterfly fly out through the window.* ORLA *and* LIAM *watch it fly away . . .*

LIAM (*concerned*). Oh. Look out for the . . .

ORLA *and* LIAM *wince . . .*

Lawnmower.

*A beat. They both stare out the window in embarrassed silence . . .* LIAM *looks down at the clapperboard.*

47 slates. Not bad for a five-day shoot.

ORLA (*getting back to work*). Let's make it 48!

> LIAM *goes back to setting up the lights.* ORLA *sets up the camera.*

You'll stay for a while and give me a hand?

LIAM (*looks at his watch*). Sure, lots of time. Shoot this scene, finish the film, call into Nicole's and shag the shit out of her.

ORLA. What do you talk about in Bakers?

LIAM. What?

ORLA. When you go for a drink with the class? What does everyone talk about?

LIAM. I don't know. Lots of things.

ORLA. Like what? Complain about lectures? Movies you like?

LIAM (*shrugs*). Yeah, that kind of thing.

ORLA. Maybe next weekend, I'll come along. I mean, what do you think?

LIAM (*working as he talks*). Yeah, you should . . .

> LIAM *positions a light stand but the DVD box on the ground is in the way. He motions to* ORLA *to move it, which she does.*

Are you planning on moving out soon?

ORLA (*shrugs*). I hadn't given it any thought. Why do you ask?

LIAM. Then why didn't you want that?

ORLA. I made a vow I wouldn't get a DVD player until I lost my virginity.

LIAM (*blankly*). I have no response to that.

> *A beat.* LIAM *goes back to setting up the equipment.* ORLA *looks at the box.*

ORLA (*cheerfully*). What the hell!

ORLA *unpacks the DVD and connects it to the television. Behind her,* LIAM *continues working.*

LIAM. Y'know what? I think I'll stay up late tonight and finish writing my script. The prawn fisher'll finally get his happy ending.

ORLA *is about to unplug the video recorder when she checks to see if there's any tape inside. She finds one and presses play.* LIAM*'s spoof video comes on.* ORLA *sits back on the sofa and watches it.*

ORLA (*on verge of tears*). When did you make this?

LIAM *goes to* ORLA *and is horrified to see what she's watching.*

LIAM. Last week. We were just messing about one afternoon. You weren't supposed to see it. I'm sorry, Orla, but it doesn't mean anything. It's just Harris didn't show up for the two o'clock lecture and Nicole read your script and . . . we were just bored. It was nothing personal though. If it was someone else's script we would have done that too. We were just having a laugh, Orla, honest. It didn't mean anything.

ORLA. Relax, Liam . . . (*She laughs, upset.*) It's only a movie.

*Lights go down.*

*The End.*

**A Nick Hern Book**

*The Gist of It* first published in Great Britain as a paperback original in 2006 by Nick Hern Books Limited, 14 Larden Road, London W3 7ST in association with Fishamble Theatre Company

*The Gist of It* copyright © 2006 Rodney Lee

Rodney Lee has asserted his right to be identified as the author of this work

Cover image: Gareth Jones

Typeset by Country Setting, Kingsdown, Kent CT14 8ES
Printed in Great Britain by Cox and Wyman Ltd, Reading, Berks

A CIP catalogue record for this book is available from the British Library

ISBN-13    978 1 85459 924 7

ISBN-10    1 85459 924 0